29 July 2011

LTG Oates,

Thanks for your leadership, mentorship and personal example.

-Bill

LEADERSHIP LAB: IRAQ

Lessons in Organizational Leadership and Counterinsurgency

William E. Benson

Raider Publishing International

New York London Cape Town

© 2010 William E. Benson

All rights reserved. No part of this book may be reproduced stored in a retrieval system or transmitted in any form by any means with out the prior written permission of the publisher, except by a reviewer who may quote brief passages in a review to be printed in a newspaper, magazine or journal.

First Printing

The views, content and descriptions in this book do not represent the views of Raider Publishing International. Some of the content may be offensive to some readers and they are to be advised. Objections to the content in this book should be directed towards the author and owner of the intellectual property rights as registered with their local government.

The views and opinions expressed in this publication are solely those of the author and do not necessarily represent the views of the United States Army or Unites States Government.

Cover images courtesy of istockphoto.com

ISBN: 978-1-61667-106-8

Published By Raider Publishing International
www.RaiderPublishing.com
New York London Cape Town
Printed in the United States of America and the United Kingdom

...to the remarkable few...

Acknowledgments

TO TARA, HANNAH, JACOB AND LEE FOR BRINGING JOY to my life.

To my mom for her encouragement.

To my dad for his sagacity and patience.

To Rob S. for his mentorship.

To Aubrey G. for his leadership.

To Mike W., Sean N., Mark B., Brian R., Ken B., Brian F., Dave S. Dan H., Mary G., Troy P., Chris V. and all the S.L. soldiers and NCOs for their professionalism, motivation and friendship.

To Dave B. for his love and support.

To all my brothers in arms for their service.

About the Cover

THE PORTRAIT OF ALEXANDER THE GREAT WAS CHOSEN FOR the cover because of his recognized abilities as a military leader and his historic attempt as the first "Western" power endeavoring to pacify the Middle East.

In 333 B.C., the twenty-three-year-old Alexander set his sights on conquering what was then referred to as Asia Minor. One of his first stops was the town of Gordium, north of Baghdad, where prophecies had foretold that whoever solved the problem of untying the Gordian knot would become the ruler of the known world.

Alexander, eager for the recognition of the oracles, journeyed to Gordium to untie the knot and be anointed as the fulfiller of the prophecy.

According to legend, after contemplating and being unable to unravel the knot, Alexander drew his sword and with decisiveness, cleaved the knot in two. The oracles immediately proclaimed the prophecy fulfilled and Alexander was on his way.

With his conviction of invincibility emboldened, Alexander and his armies rolled east, subduing nations and city-states along the way. By the time his armies had reached the Hydaspes River, inside present day India, they were exhausted and overextended. By 325 B.C., Alexander paused to consolidate his gains and unify his expansive empire. A critical element of this unification effort was the integration of Macedonian and Persian political, economic, military and cultural systems.

In 323 B.C., as Alexander was contemplating the conquest of the Arabian Peninsula, he was stricken with fever and died. His work of conquest and consolidation quickly unraveled as his efforts to unify the Macedonian and Persian people under one ruler proved impracticable.

Alexander's decisive use of the sword to solve the problem of the Gordian knot and claim the prophecy as his own at least portends the use of the sword (military might) over less violent and irreversible options. While Alexander was successful as the first "Western" leader to conquer the Middle East, his experiment at assimilating two disparate cultures did not survive his death and arguably helped sow the seeds of acrimony that has lasted millennia.

These lessons of Alexander the Great may prove prescient today as the balance of military, diplomatic, informational and economic power are applied to the West's most recent attempt to assimilate, or at least co-opt the nations and people of the Middle East. Only time will tell.

Author's Note

THIS BOOK SETS OUT TO DRAW LESSONS IN ORGANIZATIONAL leadership from the experiences of one U.S. Army Battalion during the first year of the U.S. conflict in Iraq. I have written this book from the perspective of a mid-grade Army officer who was not privy to the inner circle decisions and deliberations of policy makers and generals. As a disclaimer, I have never served on a General's staff or even spent much time outside of a battalion during my three tours in Iraq. I have, however, over the course of the war presented briefings, participated in discussions and/or attended meetings with many of the principle architects of U.S. strategy, including MNF-I and MNC-I commanders, the former Secretary of Defense, the former U.S. Ambassador to Iraq and various state department officials and contractors. That said, I don't have any special knowledge or insider information regarding higher-level decisions or strategies, nor is that the subject of this writing.

The book focuses on the first year of the war, specifically the beginnings of the insurgency from the end of June 2003 to March of 2004, but its tendrils reach into the later years of the conflict. Many of the conclusions and lessons learned emerged only after a long period of reflection; especially as the U.S. role in Iraq was winding down. The book is not intended to be a war memoir or a personal vetting, though personal opinions certainly seep through. It is an attempt at an objective telling of how one battalion developed and fought a counterinsurgency campaign for which it was mostly untrained. As you will see this was accomplished largely through the recurring Army tradition of discovery learning.

The fact that there is little discussion about actual combat is hopefully indicative of the book's intent. This is not a book on combat. In fact, despite three tours in Iraq and withstanding several close calls from enemy attacks, I have never fired my weapon at another individual. There were several times when I thought I would have to, and many times I wish I could have, but the enemy never presented himself so overtly.

While the locations discussed in the book are accurate there are no names of U.S. officers, soldiers or units listed. This was done purposefully so as not to fix blame or create an environment where people would feel the need to defend themselves or refute certain facts. The information presented is taken from my journal and notes and is given to my best recollection. There is no assertion that every event is somehow verifiable; that is not the point of the book. The U.S. military members who are discussed in the book or who are indirectly referenced will easily recognize themselves and the situations described. For everyone else, hopefully, it doesn't matter.

None of the Iraqi names used in the book are genuine. They have all been changed in an attempt to protect their identities. Several of those described have already been killed and Iraq remains a dangerous enough place that I do not wish to put others at risk.

The book is full of acronyms and military jargon. A glossary is provided for reference. Much of the military specific language was left intentionally to give the reader a feel for the culture of the Army. The dialogue was deliberately left a bit vague. While military readers should be able to follow along quite easily, I felt it important to give the uninitiated a feel for the rhythm of Army communications. None of the dialogue is exact. It was written down, as were the stories, from notes and memory.

To help clear up any confusion for non-military readers,

a brief explanation of military vocabulary is needed to clarify the roles and responsibilities of the primary characters portrayed in the book. Military call signs are used throughout the book to identify individuals, especially during dialogue and radio transmissions. The Army uses call signs to easily and clearly communicate without having the burden of remembering or correctly pronouncing names over the radio. The first word of a call sign designates the unit to which the person belongs. This is followed by one or two numbers designating the position the individual holds in the unit. In this case "Bear" refers to a battalion task force. The number 6 is used to designate the commanding officer. So when the moniker "Bear 6" is used, it is referring to the Task Force Bear Commander (a lieutenant colonel). The call sign "Apache 6" in this case represents the Apache Company Commander. In the military, the commander is responsible for all that his organization accomplishes or fails to accomplish. He is the principle decision maker for the organization and normally has the most military education and experience among the officers in his unit.

The character "Bear 3" is the operations officer (a major). The operations officer is responsible for planning, synchronizing and sometimes orchestrating operations for the commander. He and the battalion executive officer are the only two other field grade officers besides the commander that are inherently part of a battalion.

"Bear 2" is the intelligence officer for Task Force Bear. The intelligence officer is normally an Army captain responsible for describing the enemy capabilities, disposition, strengths and weaknesses. In Iraq, many battalion intelligence officers took on the added responsibility of processing detainees and evidence, conducting tactical questioning and piecing together the ambiguous tribal and familial relationships that affected operations.

Qualifying statement: There are no absolutes in fighting an insurgency. A technique that works well in one area may have the opposite effect in another. It follows then that none of the tactics or procedures written about in this book should be taken as universally true or applicable. Hopefully they foster a dialogue and highlight connections and implications on the application and execution of counterinsurgency strategies. The leadership lessons are my own.

Maps and Charts

Map of Iraq

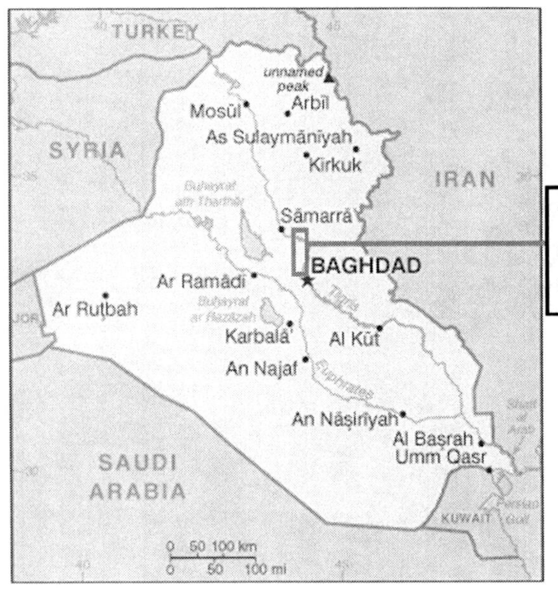

Task Force Bear approximate area of responsibility

Task Force Bear Operational Sketch

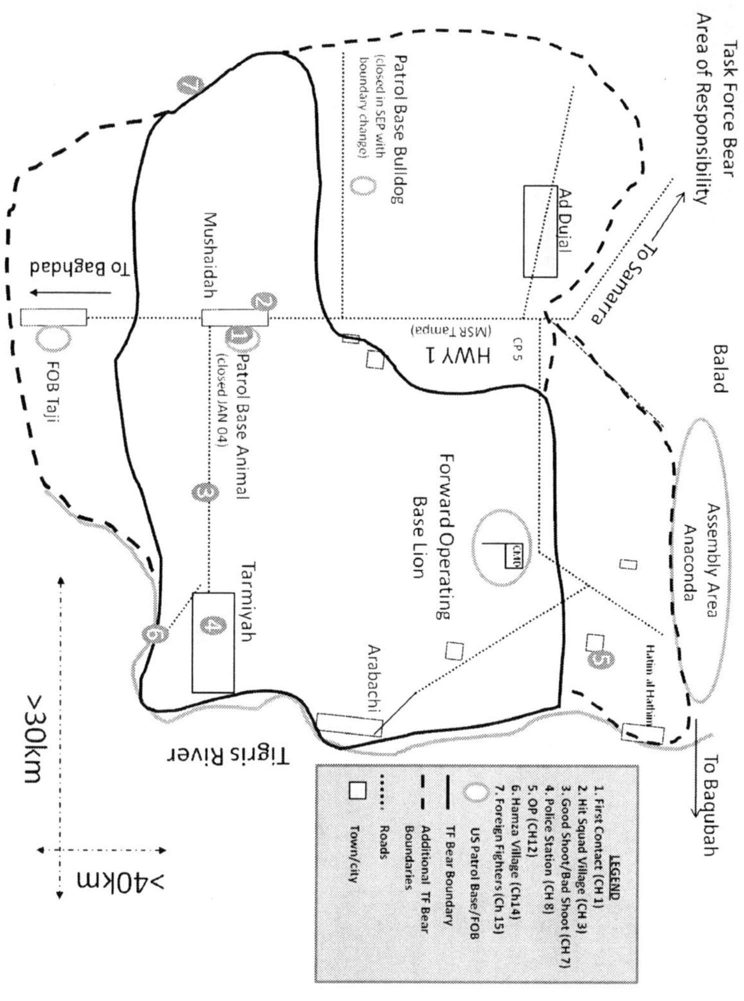

TF Bear Combat Power

Snapshot (as of 21-Oct-03)

Alpha Tank	1x Tank Platoon (<16 Soldiers) – 24 hour Quick Reaction Force for HWY 1 at Patrol Base Animal
	1x Tank Platoon (<16 Soldier) – Counter- IED patrols and flash checkpoints
	1x Tank Platoon (<16 Soldiers) - Available for on order missions
	1x Infantry Platoon (<36 Soldiers) – 24 hour Patrol Base Animal security
Bravo Tank	1x Tank Platoon (<16 Soldiers) - Iraqi Civil Defense Forces Training
	1x Tank Platoon (<16 Soldiers) – 24 hour counter-mortar OP/patrol vic AA Anaconda
	1x Tank Platoon (<16 Soldiers) – 24 hour Quick Reaction Force at FOB Lion
Bravo Infantry	1x Infantry Platoon (<36 Soldiers) – 24 hour Tarmiyah police station security and patrols
	1x Infantry Platoon (<36 Soldiers) – 24 hour Tarmiyah police station security and patrols
	1x Infantry Platoon (<36 Soldiers) – available for on order missions
Mortars	1x Platoon (approximately 15 Soldiers) – 24 hour counter-battery/patrol base security
Scouts	1x Platoon (<30 Soldiers) – on order missions, convoy security/route security/wheeled QRF
Engineers	1x Platoon (approximately 12x Soldiers as of 03 OCT) – 24 hour gate guard/prisoner guard/patrol base security

This depiction of combat power identifies the specified tasks for the various platoons of Task Force Bear. Actual numbers of Soldiers available for combat missions were often less than shown due to injury, sickness, emergency leave, work details and other competing priorities. What is not shown is all of the ancillary tasks that must be accomplished by all military units in the field. Feeding, fueling, hauling or burning trash, cleaning latrines, recovering unexploded ordinance and guarding local hire workers all competed for resources. Not to mention the need to maintain military training in skills like marksmanship, vehicle gunnery and small unit tactics.

TF Bear Combat Power

Snapshot (as of 15–JAN–04)

Alpha Tank	1x Tank Platoon (<16 Soldiers) – 24 hour Quick Reaction Force for HWY 1 at Patrol Base Animal
	1x Tank Platoon (<16 Soldier) – 24 hour availability counter- IED patrols and flash checkpoints
	1x Tank Platoon (<16 Soldiers) – 24 hour availability for area security missions and patrols around Tarmiyah
	1x Infantry Platoon (<36 Soldiers) – 24 hour Patrol Base Animal security, counter-mortar ambush
Bravo Tank	1x Tank Platoon (<16 Soldiers) - Iraqi Civil Defense Forces Training, limited patrolling
	1x Tank Platoon (<16 Soldiers) – 24 hour gate guard/prisoner guard/patrol base security
	1x Tank Platoon (<16 Soldiers) – 24 hour quick reaction force at FOB Lion
Mortars	1x Platoon (approximately 15 Soldiers) – 24 hour patrol base security/counter-battery/ other on order missions
Scouts	1x Platoon (<30 Soldiers) – 24 hour availability for on order missions, wheeled quick reaction force

This chart represents the low point in available combat power for the Task Force. Though there are considerably fewer Soldiers and platoons available in January 2004 than in October 2003 there was no corresponding reduction in the number of tasks that had to be accomplished. This shortage of combat power often led to delaying operations for lack of troops and accepting increased levels of risk in places like Tarmiyah.

Background

TASK FORCE (TF) BEAR OPERATED NORTH OF BAGHDAD as part of a Brigade Combat Team assigned to Multi-National Division North during Operation Iraqi Freedom One. When the TF first moved south from Tuz, Iraq, into the Tarmiyah area on 25 June 2003, it consisted of two armor companies, one infantry company, a headquarters company (scout and mortar platoons), a separate infantry platoon, a howitzer battery, an engineer platoon, and a civil affairs (CA) team. The TF later lost the howitzer battery, separate infantry platoon and engineer platoon; and the infantry company was detached from December through the end of February 2004, leaving the Task Force at one point with only nine platoons to conduct operations.

Task Force Bear's area of responsibility was, at its largest, spread over 1,200 square kilometers and was split by Highway 1, the primary north-south main supply route in Iraq. The main population center was the town of Tarmiyah, an outlying agrarian suburb of the Baghdad Governate with an estimated population of 150,000. The AOR also included an area south of the Balad Airfield (LSA ANACONDA) that belongs to the Sa ala Din Province. With the exception of Highway 1 and a few paved roads, the area is dominated by irrigation canals and dirt roads. The region is host to the homes and farms of a large number of high-ranking Ba'athists, including "Chemical Ali" and others directly related to the former dictator. The population is highly tribal and generally unwilling to work with the Coalition, unless coerced (money, force, shame). During the entire stay in Tarmiyah no local leader came forward with relevant information about enemy attackers or networks.

The enemy conducted over two hundred and fifty attacks in the AOR from 26 June 2003 through March 2004. These included mortar and rocket attacks on U.S. bases; rocket-propelled grenade (RPG) and small arms ambushes and improvised explosive device (IEDs) attacks. In addition to attacks on Coalition forces, the insurgents targeted contractors, police, local leaders, and soldiers of the Iraqi Civil Defense Corps (ICDC).

The types of missions Task Force Bear conducted included raids, cordon and searches, area security, route security, area and route reconnaissance, and mounted and dismounted ambushes. The primary tactical task assigned was to secure MSR Tampa (highway 1) with the purpose of allowing freedom of movement to Coalition Forces logistics patrols moving to LSA Anaconda and points north.

The TF detained over seven hundred Iraqis and killed or wounded an unknown number during its nine months around Tarmiyah. Additionally, the TF spent nearly two million dollars rebuilding sixteen schools and improving irrigation capacity. The Task Force also spent time and effort reforming the local government (replacing a number of city councilmen, mayors, ministry workers, and police), and recruiting and training new government officials, local police and more than two hundred Iraqi Civil Defense Corps (ICDC) soldiers.

The conditions experienced by the soldiers and Leaders of Task Force Bear are typical of those endured by most other battalions operating in Iraq in 2003 and early 2004.

LEADERSHIP LAB, IRAQ

Lessons in Organizational Leadership and Counterinsurgency

William E. Benson

Contents

1

First Contact

"BEAR 6", THE TASK FORCE COMMANDER, HIS OPERATIONS officer "Bear 3" and intelligence officer "Bear 2" leaned against their HMMWV; tired but pumped up after returning to the attack position from a successful early morning mission; their first as the command group for Task Force Bear. The spot was thought to be relatively secure. It was an old, destroyed Baath party compound positioned along Highway 1, the main highway running north to south in Iraq. They were at ease, helmets off, waiting for the special operations soldiers to join them for an after action review (AAR) on the recently completed operation.

Most of the soldiers present had never heard a rocket propelled grenade in flight before, let alone multiple RPGs. It's a very distinct sound, leaving no doubt as to what it was. The group actually had time to turn and watch the smoke trail from one of the projectiles as it passed within twenty meters and exploded in the median of the nearby highway. There were multiple rockets launched, but only one explosion. The command group immediately broke up with Bear 6 heading in the direction the RPGs were fired from intending to gain contact with the enemy. Bear 3 moved out to check on possible casualties and find the subordinate commanders to organize a defense. He remembers thinking "shit this is real" and being both mad that someone was shooting at them and distressed/saddened at the reality that the coming fight would most likely bring casualties. What he found surprised and angered him, but for different reasons.

The first group of soldiers he encountered were sitting on the back ramp of their infantry fighting vehicle, gear off, eating MREs. Bear 3 was incredulous. Everywhere there were soldiers not taking any action. Some were hunkered down inside the back of their armored vehicles, others were simply milling about, not sure what had happened and not sure what to do. After some choice words, the soldiers started donning their gear and Bear 3 hurried off in search of some leadership. There was an M88 with a damaged final drive that could not move on its own power, "get this thing hooked up to tow." They needed to be ready to move now. What if this was just the beginning of a determined, multi-phased attack? Finding one of the company executive officers, he charged him with getting accountability of his soldiers and getting his equipment prepared to move.

Bear 3 scrambled from place to place discovering that no one seemed to know what had happened, where the attack had come from or what action was being taken. He couldn't find the company commanders, two of which should have been nearby. As he began to make his way in the direction he believed the Task Force Commander had headed there was finally some movement. Tanks and infantry fighting vehicles began to clear the ground in the direction from which the RPGs were fired.

Inside the compound, which was serving as the attack position and assembly area, was a bombed out, three story, Ba'ath party HQ building. It dominated the surrounding terrain. The task force had been occupying the site for almost eight hours. At the base of the building there was a knot of twenty plus soldiers all peeking around the corner.

*"What the f*** is going on?"*

"RPG fire from right over there, sir."

"You saw them fire?"

"Saw the smoke trails and some guys duck behind the

low wall." He pointed to a spot maybe fifty meters away.

"So what are we doing about it? Did anyone return fire?"

Silence.

"Who's got overwatch of the site? Who's up in the building?"

Silence.

*"Who the f*** cleared this building? We have no one up on the third floor?"*

No response.

"Get a team in there now. I want overwatch and comms [communications] *up there now."*

Minutes later the Bradleys and tanks were starting to make progress clearing the ground to the front. They were perpendicular to the low wall, where the RPGs had been fired from-negative contact

"Look, the Brads have cleared forward. Take a squad and clear that wall... Let's move."

The shooters were gone. The Battalion finished clearing the ground out to five hundred meters, accounted for personnel and equipment and headed north on MSR Tampa back to base. The Special Forces soldiers had apparently not hung around either, and without even radio contact had left on their own.

Task Force Bear was lucky to survive first contact. One of the RPGs hit squarely in the back of a cargo HMMWV with three soldiers sitting in the back on the bench seats. The RPG hit the tailgate and fell harmlessly to the ground. If it had detonated, all three soldiers likely would have been killed. As was a frequent occurrence early in the war, the enemy had armed the rocket, but not the warhead. The ineffectiveness of RPGs during the summer of 2003 was so prolific that the enemy became convinced for a time that the U.S. Army had some kind of magnetic force field around their vehicles. Most often, as in this case, it was their own poor training that accounted for the misses. With the warhead unarmed the weapon was little more than a heavy, fast moving, modern day arrow. After falling to the ground it could be picked up and moved with little risk.

This first experience with enemy contact offered some crucial insight into the readiness of Task Force Bear. Its soldiers and leaders needed to fix things or soldiers were going to end up dead. Most importantly was the failure of anyone to fire a round at the attackers despite several soldiers witnessing the attack. There was also the slow response of the tank and Bradley crews, the failure to clear and put an OP on the Baath party building during the occupation of the attack position and the general apathy of the soldiers to take action, any action. From an organizational standpoint the deficiencies were compounded by the fact that many of its key leaders, and all of the company commanders had just recently been replaced; meaning that many of the leaders that had taken Task Force Bear through its initial push up through Baghdad, Taji and on to Kirkuk had been replaced by others who hadn't yet had contact with the enemy. At the time this change out of leadership was the norm across Iraq as the Army stuck to its planned leader rotations to fill schools and other career enhancing positions. Much of the leadership, who had trained and deployed with Task Force Bear, and fought with them during the initial invasion, were no longer in charge. This led to a steep learning curve for all involved. The ineptness of the enemy in mid 2003 was perhaps the most important contributor to the low number of initial casualties. Unfortunately, as the insurgency later matured, the insurgents became more effective; the stupid ones being culled as the rules of Darwinism were ruthlessly applied.

Task Force Bear's deficiencies, namely the hesitation to shoot or take immediate action during unexpected contact, were fixed in part by getting soldiers comfortable working with and firing their weapons. Abandoned buildings and unpopulated areas were identified as convenient for conducting impromptu live fire exercises. By constructing ranges and test fire areas soldiers started shooting personal and crew served weapons daily. It became normal to shoot. Soldiers, particularly tankers and support troops, became more comfortable with their personal weapons.

The pre-OIF armor battalion was simply not trained or proficient in returning small arms fire. Among most soldiers outside special operations and light infantry units, returning accurate small arms fire was not a conditioned response. It needed to be in order to fight the low tech, mostly dismounted enemy found in Iraq. Most mechanized units of the "heavy" Army spent the preponderance of their time on maintenance and "big gun" (i.e. tank and Bradley) gunnery. The emphasis on small arms proficiency and small unit, dismounted battle drills did not proliferate throughout the Army until the years immediately following 2003.

The emphasis on returning small arms fire coupled with the significant increase of soldiers with combat experience ensured that failure to return fire did not become an enduring problem in subsequent deployments. (note: On the contrary, for many units hyper vigilance and poor discipline often led soldiers to shoot too quickly, resulting in civilian casualties thereby further alienating the population)

Leadership Lessons

- *As a new leader don't assume subordinates will act as you anticipate (e.g. that soldiers will return fire when fired upon) simply because it is part of their job description. Subordinates will not react the way you expect unless they have been trained or given the opportunity to develop the appropriate conditioned response.*
- *If you are new to an organization and haven't personally witnessed proficiency in a task you consider*

critical to mission success, schedule an opportunity to train or observe the task-make your subordinates perform the task to your satisfaction.

- *Even with training and experience leaders are still needed to initiate movement.*

2

Planning

IN THE DAYS PRECEDING FIRST CONTACT, TASK FORCE BEAR had prepared for its mission through application of the Army's deliberate planning process. It was still early in the war and the U.S. was continuing to work through its "deck of cards", delineating the fifty-two most wanted ex-Iraqi government leaders. The target of this most recent raid was an associate and purported safe house of the notorious Saddam Hussein henchman, Chemical Ali. The mission was a Task Force 989 (special operations task forces were usually designated by numbers) operation with traditional special forces and other civilian three letter agencies in support. The Battalion would provide the outer cordon and service a secondary target while a ranger assault force would go after the main objective. It was the Battalion's first inter-agency mission, the first against a former member of Saddam's regime and the first for many of the leaders in their current positions. They were all eager to see how they and their unit would perform.

From receipt of the mission there were over seventy-two hours before execution. This was plenty of time to apply the military decision making process. The Task Force 989 representatives provided details on the targets and outlined what they needed in support. The battalion would support the mission with a tank company and the scout platoon occupying blocking positions on the outer cordon, and an infantry company simultaneously raiding a secondary objective. There would also be a QRF as well as forward positioned maintenance and medical assets on standby. The forward command post would be centrally located to provide command and control. Bear 6 would accompany the assault force to the secondary objective. Command and control aircraft and an air weapons team would fly overhead with fast movers (most likely air force F16s) in support in case of a troops in contact (TIC) situation. Time on target was scheduled for 0100 hours.

During the planning process information was shared with the special operations task force on the best routes to use in order to reach the primary objective, as well as the timing of the operation and the capabilities of the battalion. Satellite imagery was used to conduct map reconnaissance and determine the best locations for the blocking positions and routes onto the objective. The special operators were determined to stay off the main roads and use a secondary trail that led into the back of the objective compound despite doubts about its trafficability. Reading imagery takes some getting used to as irrigation canals and secondary roads often look similar. Ground reconnaissance while always preferred was not always feasible for fear of giving away the mission.

The planning process culminated in a sand table rehearsal that would have made a Ranger instructor proud. The rehearsal covered enemy and friendly actions by critical event, medical and logistics contingencies and spent considerable time on actions on contact. The sand table was a scale model of the operation big enough for the participants to stand and move on as they briefed their role in the mission. Except for the Special Operations Task Force being unable to attend, all other participants were present and fully prepared. It was 1400 hours. SP to the attack position would occur in eight hours.

The primary risk associated with the operation was getting ambushed during movement to the attack position along MSR Tampa. At this point in the war a direct fire attack was most likely, but use of an artillery shell or other explosive rigged to detonate on a passing vehicle was also possible (they hadn't started calling them IEDs yet). B Company had been engaged in a number of direct fire ambushes along the planned route during the previous two weeks so the threat was very real. Unfortunately it was the only route that supported the twenty-five kilometers movement to the attack position. If contact did occur along the route, the plan called for the element in contact to return fire and develop the situation until the QRF moved forward to assume the fight, allowing the attack column to continue its movement. Medical and recovery assets were incorporated into the movement and damaged vehicles would be recovered back to the FOB or forward to the attack position based on a break point along the route. Maintaining momentum was important with over forty vehicles in the movement, fifty meters between vehicles and two hundred meters between serials. The column would be spread out over several kilometers.

Everything went as planned and on time up to and including occupation of the attack position; a major accomplishment as this was the Battalion's first attempt at this type of operation under the unit's new leadership. The command and control (C2) element from the special operations task force arrived at the attack position shortly after to conduct final coordination. Since the special operators had missed the rehearsal there were several details about march speed and sequencing of the various elements that needed to be worked out. At 0030 hours the lead infantry platoon lined up in its M2 BFVs. At 0040 hours movement was initiated to the start point (SP) while the lead elements of the special operations task force moved up route Tampa from the South. The plan had the special operators executing the SP at 0100 with lead vehicles from TF Bear following close behind. As with most plans this one didn't survive past the line of departure

(LD).

There was some confusion by the lead Task Force Bear element as to the SP sequence. When they were told to move they continued through the SP making a left onto Route Cobra instead of pausing for the special operations assault force to take lead. Following close behind, the Bear 3 and special operations command and control element realized simultaneously that they had gone too early. Instead of being just behind the ground assault force they were now leading a column of tanks, Bradleys and HMMWVs stretching over several kilometers with the Task Force 989 assault force element still moving towards the SP from the South. The lead special operator of the C2 element was not happy:

"We've gone too far... They already hit the SP... What are they doing?"

"Bravo Red 1, this is Bear 3. You've gone too far."

"This is Bravo Red 1. Negative. We are on the route."

"Roger. But you need to be behind the Black (special operations task force) element. They haven't hit the SP yet."

At that moment the TF 989 C2 element HMMWV pulled up alongside Bear 3. No one had doors on so the special operator in the right hand seat of his HMMWV yelled across Bear 3's driver as the vehicles continued to move down the road.

*"What the f***. I think you already hit the SP."*

"I know."

"We need to get them turned back around and wait at the SP. Any Bear element this is Black 2-4." (This was the first radio contact from the ranger assault force.)

"Black 2-4, this is Bear 3."

"Roger, Bear 3. We are moving north on Tampa 3 k south of CP 31."

"Roger, 2-4."

From the TF 989 C2 element: *"Get your unit f****** turned around."*

"If we turn around now, we'll just get in the way (getting an armored column turned around on a two lane road in the middle of the night with unseasoned troops is always an experiment) *we need to just pull off and let them pass."*

"Bravo Red 1, this is Bear 3. Stop your move. Stop your move and pull off the road."

"Roger, Bear 3."

*"I said get this f****** unit turned around. You're going to f*** up the entire op. This is your f****** fault."*

"We don't have time."

*"Bull****. Get them f****** turned around."*

"...OKAY but this is your call."

"Bravo Red 1, this is Bear 3. We need to move back to the SP and let the Black element get by."

"This is Red 1. Roger."

"Bear 3, this is Black 2-4 we just hit the SP. Is this you on the route?"

"Roger. We're getting out of the way," he said as he switched handmikes, *"all elements this net stop your move, get off the route and turn off your lights, I say again get off the route and turn off your lights, the assault force is moving through."*

The C2 element yelled, *"This is f***** up."*

"Black 2-4, the route is clear for you; break, Red 1 prepare to move behind Black 2-4."

It worked. The ground assault force made up of Rangers in their modified HMMWVs moved through at a high rate of speed. The rest of Task Force Bear was back on timeline. The only problem now was keeping up with the trail vehicle of Rangers, which was quickly distancing itself.

"Red, this is Bear 3. Move... You need to keep eyes on their trail vehicle; remain blackout. I say again: All elements remain blackout."

Maintaining contact with the trail vehicle was easier said than done. The Rangers were moving out quickly. The lead platoon only briefly got eyes on the rear vehicle of the assault force as they careened down a secondary route towards the objective. During the movement Bear 3 moved up to the third vehicle spot to get better control of the forward movement. He was determined not to make another mistake.

The column hit the release point (RP) and split to occupy various blocking positions. For some this meant another twelve kilometers of movement before being set. The lead elements moving with Bear 3 needed to move through the center of town to reach their positions. They weren't sure what to expect. So far there had been only limited engagement with the locals and little intelligence on the area. All that was known was that Tarmiyah was a supposed vacation spot for many of the high ranking Sunni, Baathist leaders from Baghdad, with nicer homes and villas spread along the nearby Tigris River.

As the lead element entered the town, inexplicably, there was a line of flames spreading across the street. The black smoke made it more difficult to see even for those equipped with night vision sights. The lead vehicle slowed.

"Bear 3, this is Red 1. We've got fire across the street."

"Keep moving. Don't stop. Don't stop," yelled Bear 3 into the hand mike and to his driver at the same time.

They were through the flames; no enemy contact, but surprisingly there were a lot of young men out on the street. In a few minutes Bear 3 and the special forces command and control element were set at the predetermined forward command post location checking off on their maps and execution checklists as the blocking positions were established. As the command and control element settled in, gunfire from multiple caliber weapons erupted periodically, and regularly could be heard in the distance. Soldiers eventually became used to this type of nuisance gunfire, but in July 2003 it was still quite unnerving. The Rangers hit their objective, so far so good. Now it was B Company's turn.

"Bulldog 6, this is Bear 3. SITREP. Over."

"This is Bulldog 6. Still moving to the objective."

Something wasn't right. The plan called for the secondary assault force to follow immediately behind the lead element and Bear 3 so it could roll directly onto its own objective. Extra dismounts had been consolidated forward in one of the 1SGs cargo HMMWVs and two M113 personnel carriers. The plan was to roll up to the house and get inside quickly; relying on the element of surprise to reduce risk. As often happens to new units in country, they missed the turn off to the objective. Not once, not twice, but three times. To make matters worse they entered the wrong house, clearing it to the roof before realizing the mistake. In a great show of initiative the soldiers simply hopped the gap between the two roofs onto the next building and cleared from top down, bagging their target without a fight. The three lettered agency folks traveling with Task Force Bear immediately went to work with field interrogation. Now it was simply waiting for the Rangers to complete their search of the primary objective.

This took much longer than expected. As one hour merged into two, patience was wearing thin. They were supposed to have been off the objective in less than twenty minutes. Now they were approaching two hours. The longer they stayed on the objective the more time the enemy would have to set up an ambush on the way out. Finally the special operators admitted what had happened. One of the Ranger HMMWVs had flipped on the way in. The route was barely trafficable, mostly cross-country. There were injuries and it had taken a long time to recover the vehicle. After over three hours, the word to move finally came. The trip back to the attack position proved uneventful save for some uncomfortable moments when vehicle movement became congested and stopped with Bear 3, now as the trail vehicle, with no doors and no crew served weapon, sitting in the middle of town, which was packed with staring, young Iraqi males barely more than an arms-length away. Fortunately, both sides were intimidated enough to keep to their own business.

The Battalion's first inter-agency raid was a success. While they hadn't found their principle target, they did take into custody a significant person of interest, who remained out of sector for weeks while he was questioned. More importantly, the Tank Battalion Task Force (Task Force Bear) demonstrated its ability to plan and execute a complex operation it had never been trained or equipped to conduct.

Before 2003 tank battalions weren't raiding houses, weren't developing targeting packets on individuals, were not routinely using imagery to plan operations, were not establishing blocking positions and C2 nodes in support of interagency missions, had not trained on Battle Drill 6 or close quarters marksmanship. Neither had they been equipped with the night vision devices, communications gear or weapons, lasers and sights normally used to conduct these missions. Not to mention the need for up-armored HMMWVs of which the Battalion had none in July 2003.

For example armor battalions and similar units didn't have MBiTR radios, the kind that allow a dismounted section to talk to the vehicles operating in support. Nor were there the needed number of night vision goggles (NVGs) let alone NVG mounts to allow soldiers to operate dismounted at night. Most nineteen series soldiers had never operated with NVGs mounted to their helmets because in a tank or Bradley night vision goggles are worn around the neck so they don't interfere with acquiring targets through the vehicle targeting and thermal sight systems.

These deficiencies would be corrected over the next six years of the conflict as the Army went through an unprecedented (at least in contemporary times) process of upgrading and outfitting the force. Certainly the ability for the Army to support its soldiers with the latest equipment is one of the greatest and least recognized achievements of the war.

As always, however, the Battalion could have done better. The two biggest mistakes were hitting the SP ahead of the Ranger assault force, and then missing the turn to the secondary objective even after multiple tries. Each of these mistakes could have jeopardized the mission and/or caused casualties if the enemy had been alert or willing to put up a fight.

During the AAR process it quickly became apparent why there was a mix up with hitting the SP. During the rehearsal no one had replicated the Ranger assault force. Even though the commander of the lead vehicle had walked the terrain model and briefed his movement he had not accounted for the Ranger assault force to his front. Because he didn't see it and account for it in the rehearsal, in his mind his vehicle remained in the lead. This was an obvious mistake. If the Ranger assault force had been replicated on the terrain board or someone had been identified to brief the Ranger's role in the operation and walk the route on during the rehearsal, the lead TF Bear element would have understood not to cross the SP until after the assault force had passed to their front. They would have understood that their move was conditions based and not tied to time.

The second problem was more difficult to fix. Finding the right road or house, at night, in unfamiliar urban terrain is always a challenge. This was long before the introduction of the ubiquitous FBCB2/BFT systems that place maps and imagery at the fingertips of every vehicle commander in Iraq. There were three things that the Task Force used to mitigate this risk in the future. First, imagery was used and distributed down to the vehicle commander level to help him better identify the correct target or route. Second, when possible local Iraqi sources were used in lead vehicles to identify the proper route or building (this was not always successful as the average Iraqi has a difficult time reading a map or imagery). Third, the Battalion immediately started an aggressive reconnaissance program to get platoons more familiar with the terrain. The reconnaissance objectives were to identify routes and restricted terrain and to classify bridges for movement of wheeled and tracked vehicles of various weights. Additionally digital photographs were taken and catalogued of all the relevant urban areas, meaning that on most subsequent missions actual photographs of the objectives in question were available. The intent was to have platoons so familiar with the area that there would never be another objective to reach that someone in the Battalion hadn't already been to or near. This would prove invaluable for future missions.

Leadership Lessons

- *When conducting rehearsals, every element that is participating in the operation must be replicated and must walk through or talk through their piece of the operation. This applies especially to attachments or elements that have not previously worked with the organization.*
- *In the absence of orders, conduct reconnaissance. You can never have enough information about your operating environment.*

3

Snipers on Rooftops

THE INTELLIGENCE THAT LEAD TO OPERATION "HIT SQUAD" came from a middle-aged Iraqi half-Kurd, a former police officer who was dismissed under Saddam Hussien for undisclosed transgressions-most notably his Kurdish ancestry. Abbas and his brother provided so much quality information that it set the foundation for Task Force Bear's understanding of the entire area as well as eight months worth of targeted operations. This included names of Ba'athist officers living in the area, those who conducted torture and arrests under Saddam Hussien, as well as information on corrupt police officers and other criminals and potential insurgent sympathizers. While the Battalion command group was initially skeptical and suspicious, and single source reporting would not survive as the standard of evidence to conduct operations, in July 2003 there was little else to go on.

The objective in question for this mission was actually three distinct homesteads spread over three square kilometers; about ten dwellings plus courtyards, outbuildings and fields. The targets were several purported Baathist torturers and toughs, though it was unclear how many would actually be on the objective. Abbas was confident that these men would be armed, that they normally posted lookouts on the roofs of their homes and may fight back. When Bear 2 presented the intelligence summary he warned of the possibility of enemy lookouts, categorizing them as snipers, on rooftops. What lent credence to the intelligence and gave the last impetus to go ahead with the operation was a direct fire ambush conducted against a B Company patrol moving south on route Tampa the week prior. Routes from the ambush site led directly back to the objective area, which also provided a canal to aid in the enemy's egress. The one wounded Iraqi left on the scene of the ambush had grabbed the muzzle of the B Company commander's weapon, stuck it to his chest and said in perfect English, "kill me". While he provided little additional information, the fact the ambush occurred so close to the suspected area, and the fact that the wounded attacker was so defiant, provided enough of a potential threat to warrant an operation.

The plan called for three columns moving independently from two different start points along three different routes to simultaneously establish a cordon, followed by a "hard" raid against the principle dwellings. The majority of the movement would be conducted at in hours of darkness. Decisive to the mission was getting the cordon set, so timing would be critical. Once set, there was confidence the enemy couldn't escape and the hope was that it wouldn't resist. The assault and cordon elements consisted of tanks, BFVs, M113s, HMMWVs and an Air Weapons Team (AWT) of two Apache helicopters. The AWT proved crucial in so many operations by providing early observation on objectives, screening flanks for potential movement on and off objectives and most importantly to provide a psychological edge against the enemy. In 2003 many Iraqis were convinced that our aircraft could see through walls and underground. Just having them in the air usually froze most who otherwise would try to escape or attack. There was also a psychological operations team that would broadcast messages to those within the houses, urging them not to resist and instructing them where to go. A tactical human intelligence team was incorporated so vetting of detainees could start immediately on the objective.

The night prior to the mission the battalion prepositioned its forces forward at two of the company patrol bases and then settled in for some fitful sleep. Soldiers rested where they could, laid out on the hoods of HMMWVs, on the decks of tanks or sitting upright, heads resting against windshields and gunner's sights. At approximately 0430 the soldiers at patrol base Bulldog heard the reports of several distant explosions. Then came the call.

"Bear X-ray, this is Apache X-ray. Over."

"This is Bear X-ray. Go ahead."

"This is Apache X-ray. Contact... Receiving incoming... Multiple rounds... Returning fire."

As elements from A company were conducting pre-combat checks for the mission a civilian pick-up truck raced by the front of their combat outpost as five Iraqis, faces covered in traditional Arab scarves, fired RPGs from the back of the truck. At least one U.S. machine gunner returned fire from the roof, but the incident was over in a matter of seconds and the pick-up truck sped off. No one was injured on the U.S. side despite several direct hits on the compound and buildings. Enemy battle damage was unknown. Everyone was on edge.

Did the enemy know of the pending operation? Were they trying to disrupt the movement? Would they be waiting to unleash an ambush as the BN moved out? The decision was quickly made to continue with the operation. SP was scheduled in just a few minutes and any delay or an uncoordinated movement would jeopardize getting the cordon set; and with any luck, the bad guys just might get caught returning home.

The three columns moved out. Each had responsibility for establishing part of the cordon as well as assaulting one of the three sub-objectives. The two tank and one infantry company commanders were in charge of the columns and would ensure that blocking positions were set and the assault forces hit the right houses. They also controlled the local reserve forces. Bear 3 and the TAC moved with the northern column. They got caught on the wrong side of one of the canals and had to quickly back up and push around but the timing wasn't significantly altered. Bear 6 moved with the main effort against the most dangerous objective. This was the objective where contact was most likely and where most of the detainees were expected. The AWT initially took up position on the western flank to screen along the most likely egress routes until the cordon was set. During the rehearsal much time was spent ensuring sectors of fire were clear so that any small arms engagement wouldn't result in friendly casualties. Assuming direct fire contact from an objective was always part of contingency planning and required detailed coordination between elements moving along convergent avenues of attack and setting numerous, non-contiguous blocking positions. No one wanted the blocking positions to turn into *de facto* backstops during a firefight. Soldiers at the blocking positions would initially remain "buttoned up" inside their armored vehicles just in case.

All three columns hit their individual RPs within one minute of each other. The assault forces were on the objectives, moving through the buildings immediately. After a brief delay the psychological operations team started broadcasting its prepared message. A recorded Arabic voice directed the men, women and children to exit their houses and congregate in the courtyards until an American arrived to give them further instructions. Best of all there was no enemy contact.

Bang!

A single shot rang out from the southern objective; B company's objective. Even from over a kilometer away Bear 3 heard the shot.

"Bulldog 6 or Bulldog 5, this is Bear 3. SITREP. Over."

Silence.

"Bulldog 6 or Bulldog 5, this is Bear 3. SITREP. Over."

More silence.

"Bear 3, this is Bulldog 5."

"SITREP. Over."

"This is Bulldog 5. Roger. Red platoon is on GOLD, executing buildings 3 and 4, negative enemy contact."

"This is Bear 3. Roger. I heard a shot from your direction over."

"This is Bulldog 5. Uhmm, no one's reported anything."

"Okay, let's find out where that shot came from."

It wasn't until the after action review (AAR) when everyone found out what had happened. On objective GOLD the plan was to simultaneously enter two building at ground level and clear upwards. Each squad had rehearsed this separately as part of their troop leading procedures. In the half-light before sunrise, as the lead infantryman reached the roof of the northern building, he looked across and saw a shape on the opposite roof holding a weapon. Having been briefed to expect enemy "snipers" on the rooftops, he immediately dropped to a knee, aimed center of mass and shot one round. The round hit the trigger mechanism of the Squad Automatic Weapon the U.S. soldier, his platoon mate, was carrying at the low ready as he assaulted onto the roof of building number three. The round damaged the weapon but did not injure the soldier. The Battalion had had another close call and again came away unscathed.

The after action review (AAR) process referred to above helped Task Force Bear learn what had happened on the objective and how to apply those lessons to ensure the same mistakes weren't made twice. In this case the AAR focused on deconflicting direct fires between adjacent objectives and reviewing the information published in the intelligence estimate that may have overstated the expected enemy threat.

The U.S. Army routinely uses the AAR process in its training regimens to capture, codify and improve on tactics, techniques and standard operating procedures at all levels. The AAR is regarded as one of the most important aspects of training; indeed many claim that without an AAR the training value of any event is negligible. The after action review process can be run internally or chaired by an outside facilitator, can be informal or formal, consist of a multimedia presentation or be conducted on site where the effects of the training or operation are still evident. The important thing is that it gets done and that the organization's leaders fully participate. The first rule of any AAR is "no thick skins".

For Task Force Bear the AAR was critical to improving the unit's performance conducting counterinsurgency operations. AARs were routinely done after every mission. When new U.S. patrol tactics proved successful or a new enemy technique was particularly effective, they were formally written into assessments that were then shared within and between units. In part, because of this process, the incident of one Task Force Bear soldier accidentally shooting another was the first and last friendly fire incident the unit had to contend with.

Leadership Lessons

- *Be realistic and mindful of the second and third order effects when describing the enemy threat to subordinates. The tendency to worst case the problem may cause unintended consequences-"snipers on rooftops".*
- *Separate elements operating on the same objective must rehearse together (see Chapter 2).*

- *Don't allow unrelated actions (RPG attack against PB Apache) to disrupt your initiative and delay your operations.*
- *After Actions Reviews are a must; especially in combat.*

4

Detainees, Part 1

THE REST OF THE OPERATION WAS UNEVENTFUL, BUT tedious. Hours were spent searching houses, fields and canals. Tactical questioning was done to all military aged males. Family members were sequestered. Some required medical attention and most needed water. A few weapons were found wrapped in plastic bags and stored underwater in irrigation canals. This lead to further searching of canals using impromptu grappling hooks and rakes. In some cases soldiers walked through water up to their chests trying to locate hidden caches of weapons. The results were disappointing.

What they did end up with was a plethora of detainees; forty-eight in all. After eight hours on the objective two five ton trucks were full of sandbag-hooded Iraqis. This was far more detainees than expected. The limited tactical questioning done at the site added to instead of reduced the number of suspects. Most surprising was that several of the Iraqis actually provided additional derogatory information about their neighbors, and in some cases their relatives, confirming that the right guys had been captured. The problem now was what to do with forty-eight detainees. There was too much corroborating evidence, and too many remaining questions to let any of them go. And in spite of some on scene confessions and revelations, there were still some detainees whose names had yet to be confirmed.

After eight hours in 115+-degree heat no one wanted to mistakenly leave a bad guy behind. So the decision was made to take them all back to the Forward Operating Based for questioning.

As the five-ton truck, loaded with nearly all the military aged males from the area backed into the northern most objective to pick up the last few detainees, a most unanticipated event occurred. The women on the objective started to wail. Not only did they wail, they beat their chests, cried and called out to their loved ones on the trucks. The oldest lady of the group suddenly fell hard, feinting and smacking her head with a loud "thwack" on the concrete. Women and children surged forward towards the trucks. Wary and reticent soldiers positioned themselves to block the women and children from getting too close. Leaders barked orders.

"Get those men loaded and get the truck out of here."

"Hey, push 'em back. Push 'em back."

"Where's the interpreter? Get him up here."

A medic quickly moved in to assist the woman who had fainted. The interpreter arrived

"Tell them it's going to be okay. Tell them its going to be okay. Tell them... Tell them that anyone who hasn't done anything wrong will be released."

Several of the Iraqi woman approached Bear 3 distraught, angry, afraid and shouted in Arabic

"When will they be back? You can't take all the men from us."

"Who will protect us?"

"You've taken all our ID cards, our ration cards. We will starve."

"What are they saying about ration cards?"

"Tell them we will look into it and bring them back their ration cards if we find them. Tell them the men will return if they are innocent."

"Just leave us Farhan. He is good. He hasn't done anything, take the rest just leave us Farhan," complained

one woman.

"Don't leave us here alone, we will starve."

The medic finished helping the older Iraqi woman who had fainted.

"The detainees are loaded."

"Okay, let's move out."

"Hey, terp [short for interpreter], *tell them nothing bad will happen to the men, if they are innocent they will come back."*

The words had little effect. The women, who had been momentarily placated, begin yelling and crying again as the trucks began to leave, several rushed forward. Bear 3 remained on the ground with a couple of soldiers to keep them from getting too close to the trucks. When the five-ton trucks had cleared the area Bear 3 and the soldiers jumped into the remaining HMMWV and headed back to base at the trail of the column. An hour later back at the FOB, the question became what to do with forty-eight detainees.

The plan had been for the informant Abbas to visit the base the day following the raid. He would identify and write sworn statements about which from among the forty-eight detainees were conducting attacks against Coalition Forces and terrorizing the locals. Known as "Fedayine Saddam", these guerilla fighters were an assorted lot of petty thugs and former Baath party officials loosely organized to continue the fight after the Iraqi Army was defeated. Taking responsibility for that many Iraqis who's guilt or innocence was still in question strained the Battalion's capabilities logistically as well as its ability to process the detainees. It often took hours of questioning just to determine accurate names. Some detainees deliberately misled by giving false names or switching names with other detainees. The experience taught some valuable lessons that quickly led to adapting new procedures.

The most important lesson was the value of questioning

as many Iraqis on the objective as possible in order to reduce the number that needed to be moved back to a U.S. FOB. This was accomplished by having the source or informant accompany the intelligence team, usually by having him wear a poncho, facemask and goggles to hide his identity. The potential detainees were then either paraded in front of the informant or pictures were taken using a digital camera and then used to separate the bad from the not so bad.

The need for local interpreters, or any interpreters, was never more evident than on an objective. It not only helped ensure the right people were detained, but also assisted in communicating with the women and children. Iraqi women actually became a surprising ally on many objectives. They were used to accompany soldiers conducting searches, would open up locked drawers and doors (eliminating the need to break them), would be given charge of the family's valuables and ID cards (the women were used to the Iraqi Army's practice of stealing from the local population and expected the same from the Americans) and often turned in their own husbands and relatives. Many Iraqi women it seemed were fed up with the actions of their husbands and they wanted them out of the picture, a practice that became increasingly more regular as the year progressed.

Another important lesson that quickly became SOP was to keep the women and children segregated from the detainee processing. Backing the five-ton truck filled with hooded and handcuffed family members up to a house undoubtedly invoked images of life under Saddam. Certainly the Iraqi women and children believed that when we took away their men, they would never be seen again. As the year progressed some of these fears were allayed as the locals became confident that their loved ones would be treated well and released if innocent. But the impact on local Iraqis at seeing their men roughly treated and hauled away in hoods and handcuffs would always be considered when planning operations in the future. Of course sometimes fear and shame is exactly the message that needs to be sent, but this should be a planned effect not an accidental one.

Leadership Lessons

- *Understand the history of the area and people you are dealing with to better understand how they may respond to your actions.*
- *Remember that actions may have undesired effects. Take into account second and third order consequences. Plan for these as part of your rehearsals and preparations. For example, the unit was unprepared for the visceral reaction from the villagers and family members seeing their male relatives blindfolded and bound. Including civilian reaction during the rehearsal would have helped plan a proper response. Another example of unexpected consequences was the hardship placed on Iraqi families when all the males were taken from their homes and their identification cards confiscated. The TF Bear leadership was initially unaware of the how the Iraqi people depended on their identification cards in order to receive their monthly ration of food. By confiscating the ID cards the TF risked alienating the population and strengthening its support for the insurgents.*

5

Detainees, Part 2

WITHOUT A DOUBT, DEALING WITH DETAINEES WAS ONE of the most challenging and potentially important tactical problems that leaders had to deal with early in the war. The basic predicament concerning detainees was the conflict between the need to exploit them for intelligence and the requirement to move them to higher HQ expeditiously. The standard for how long a detainee could remain at battalion level before moving to higher HQ shifted over time, but pretty early on was set at forty-eight hours. A brigade or division commander could approve an exception to the forty-eight-hour requirement for intelligence or security reasons, and there were other nuanced circumstances and considerations that influenced how detainees were processed.

While soldiers and officers could tactically question detainees, they could not interrogate them. By Army regulation, only trained interrogators are allowed to conduct interrogations. The difference: tactical questioning involves only direct questioning. For example: "What is your name?" "Do you know Ahmed Mohammed?" Interrogation on the other hand includes various techniques designed to coerce information out of an individual. These techniques include stress positions, sleep deprivation and working threats and shame into a line of questioning to evoke a response. Only trained interrogators are authorized to use these types of interrogation techniques. They are explicitly forbidden for use by the rank and file soldiers and officers that make up the rest of the Army. While these delineations in interrogation authority became clearly understood by all over time, early in the war things were more ambiguous. In fact, at the beginning of the conflict, some battalion level intelligence officers and NCOs received familiarization training on some of the controlled interrogation techniques discussed above. The intent was to give officers and NCOs at the battalion level an expanded capability to harvest information from detainees. But by late 2003, as rumors about the soon to be revealed Abu Gahreb scandal started to circulate, strict policies governing the mandatory movement of detainees away from battalions were enacted and enforced.

The complexities that affected a leader's decision on moving detainees from a battalion to a brigade or higher level holding area were many. They included the battalion's ability to properly house and care for the detainees, the need to exploit detainees for intelligence and information, the capability of the unit and the inherent risk involved with physically moving the detainees to another location, the amount of time it took to process detainees and fill out the required data in the detention paperwork (it sometimes took hours of questioning just to figure out a detainees name), the risk involved with having some type of detrimental incident (a la Abu Gahreb-the infamous event regarding the abuse of Iraqi prisoners at the hands of American soldiers that were photographed and subsequently released to the world) and the very real possibility that many of the detainees were innocent and should really be set free. In reality, the forty-eight-hour time requirement to move detainees to a higher headquarters inhibited the ability for battalions to properly vet a population of forty-eight, sixty or eighty detainees. This was especially true when operating in a new area and was compounded by the acute shortage of interpreters in mid 2003. There was also the very real problem of determining how many of the detainees were actual bad guys in need of being taken off the street and how many were simply in the wrong place at the wrong time.

This problem was exacerbated by the fact that in 2003 most army interrogators had little experience dealing with insurgents and most had never actually interrogated anyone. A twenty-year-old American, school-trained "interrogator" rarely has the life experience, requisite cultural awareness or self-confidence to effectively interrogate a forty year old Iraqi Arab tribal leader. Their life experiences are too distinct.

The bottom line, at least for Task Force Bear, was that little to no useable intelligence was ever gleaned by U.S. Army interrogators conducting formal interrogations, and once a detainee was transferred to a higher level detainee center no useful information ever came back. The decision to move a detainee higher was therefore a deliberate, carefully examined proposition.

From July 2003 until March of 2004 the Task Force detained over seven hundred Iraqis. That averages out to over sixty a month or more than two a day. In this case, "detained", meant being transported back to the Battalion holding area and processed by the Battalion intelligence officer. Of the seven hundred Iraqis detained, well over fifty percent were released for lack of evidence. This resulted in a relatively low percentage of detainees actually moving to a higher-level detention facility compared to many other battalions. The relatively low percentage was due to several factors. Among the most important was the decision made by Task Force Bear leadership to conduct in depth tactical questioning and when possible actual interrogations using a Tactical Human Intelligence Team at the battalion level. This often meant asking for exception to the forty-eight-hour policy in order to hold on to detainees for as long as possible. Task Force Bear took this approach with the hope of harvesting the most useable intelligence while also insuring only the enemy, and not innocent civilians, became part of the coalition detention system.

While most detainees spent only a few days in the TF Bear holding area, some spent over a week, and in a few cases several weeks as interrogation and tactical questioning continued. The benefits to this were twofold. First, the information gathered on the area and its personalities, its tribes and insurgent groups led directly to the Battalion's ability to conduct precise, targeted operations. These precise operations ensured the Battalion was able to avoid conducting big "sweeps" where large numbers of military aged males were detained. Secondly, by keeping the detainees in the local holding area, the unit of capture (in this case TF Bear) gained the advantage of having local Iraqi leaders present themselves in order to negotiate for the detainees' release. This negotiation proved one of the most frequent points of departure for conversation and contact with local leaders that eventually engendered more meaningful relationships.

On a larger scale the MNC-I policy of "send everyone detained to the next higher-level holding area within forty-eight hours and let the 'professional interrogators' figure out who should be released" directly contributed to the overcrowding of prisons that resulted in some of the abuses exposed in the Abu Gahreb debacle. By holding detainees for a longer period Task Force Bear released those it found to be little threat or those who would be of better value to the Task Force back out in the community. The Task Force accumulated "wasta" (aka respect/influence) with the local population because the local Iraqi Sheiks and leaders had faith that innocent Iraqis would be released. This, in turn, directly improved the security situation in the area because the local population did not fear abuse at the hands of Task Force Bear. In the most successful example of intelligence gained through these methods was of the young Iraqi who voluntarily remained in the detention facility and reported on conversations other detainees were having. The intelligence gained from this effort lead directly to several operations that disrupted or eliminated insurgent cells that were distributing rocket launchers and munitions across Iraq. (See Chapter 14.)

Under the best of circumstances, life for a detainee was unpleasant— for many, deservedly so. After being pulled from their homes, and in some cases their beds, usually at night, zip-stripped and blindfolded, stuffed into the back of a truck or helicopter and driven or flown from their home for up to an hour, offloaded by rough hands at an undisclosed location this proved a truly terrifying experience. As many can attest it was not unusual for those detained to defecate or piss themselves during transport.

In the case of TF Bear, detainees were kept in the looted and decrepit four-room building next to the FOB's entry control point. When this area first started being used there were no doors on the rooms; soldiers had boarded up the windows with plywood. Hastily emplaced concertina wire provided the only barriers to the entrance/exit. There was no air conditioning or other accoutrements like sleeping mats or blankets. At night the temperature rarely got below 100 degrees Fahrenheit. Detainees were packed into small rooms, with barely enough space to lie down and sleep. As tough as these conditions were they were not dissimilar to how most American soldiers were living in the summer of 2003.

Perhaps most dangerous was the fact that the detainees were often guarded by the very soldiers who had captured them. This was especially problematic if the capture followed an attack that had caused American casualties. All the ingredients existed for a potential catastrophe. Overcrowding, terrified detainees, aggressive young soldiers untrained in detainee procedures looking to avenge a fallen comrade, lack of sleep, high stress and inadequate facilities. These conditions were the norm rather than the exception in the summer of 2003. It led some battalions to decide it wasn't worth keeping detainees at all, sending them higher as soon as they were captured. Others, like Task Force Bear, fought to keep detainees longer in order to gain more time sensitive information and make sure innocent Iraqis were not interred; implicitly accepting the risk of a potential Abu Gahreb like incident.

The sad but incredibly simple truth about the incidents of detainee abuse that occurred in Iraq early in the war is how easily each could have been stopped without trials or investigations or recriminations, and without press involvement. All that was needed was a leader to say, "Stop." Arguably the single most damaging event to U.S. policy objectives in Iraq— Abu Gahreb— could have and should have been stopped by the first sergeant or lieutenant or leader in the chain of command. This is not to absolve more senior leaders from responsibility. For any Army leader involved in the questioning, interrogating or housing of a prisoner to abrogate responsibility for the care of those prisoners is disingenuous at best. The argument that "I wasn't trained" or that it "wasn't in my job description" runs contrary to how Army leaders are taught and trained to take charge and accept responsibility regardless of the circumstances. The fact is that many if not most soldiers and leaders during OIF 1 were executing tasks that they weren't specifically trained for. Tankers and engineers were riding around on HMMWVs conducting dismounted raids, artillerymen were conducting civil military operations, infantrymen were training police, Army officers and NCOs of all branches and ranks were running local governments and providing essential services. Army leaders are trained to make assessments, develop courses of action, make recommendations/decisions and then take action. The "I wasn't trained" argument is an excuse that shouldn't fly.

As already alluded to, there were certainly detainee abuses that occurred at the battalion level and below early in the war. Many of these have been well documented in the press and prosecuted in the military court system. There were also practices such as putting detainees to work filling sandbags or picking up trash, or leading them through physical training that proliferated across Iraq in the summer of 2003. While not abusive, these practices were stopped as policies governing the appropriate treatment of detainees were articulated. What is clear is that the vilification of U.S. soldiers and the Army goes far beyond what most other countries would subject their own forces to. In truth the fact there weren't more incidents given the conditions and environment U.S. soldiers were placed in is a testament to their values and upbringing as Americans as well as the Army's discipline and leadership, especially at the junior levels.

In the case of the Task Force Bear, as in most battalions, it was the leaders that set the tone for how detainees were treated. The commander and field grade officers and the senior non-commissioned officers routinely sat in on tactical questioning, visited the holding areas on a daily basis, talked to the guard force and made sure living conditions were improved to meet standards. Through their actions and words they established an atmosphere of firm but fair treatment for detainees. As Task Force Bear's reputation for fair treatment spread, a significant dividend of goodwill was returned from the local population. If soldiers or leaders strayed toward the line of unacceptable treatment of detainees out of frustration, anger or overzealousness, they were corrected and counseled before the treatment got out of hand. Guards and leaders were rotated so resentments wouldn't fester. The Task Force doctor checked for medical issues, and local Iraqi leaders were occasionally allowed to visit the detainees. How to process, question and care for large numbers of detainees wasn't anything the leaders or soldiers of Task Force Bear were trained to do but it was something that needed to be done.

Leadership Lessons

- *Never forget the maxim of the strategic corporal which teaches that even the most junior leader can have strategic impact (think about the consequences of Abu Gahreb) through what they do or, as importantly, don't do.*
- *Leaders can delegate authority but never their responsibility.*
- *Lack of training or experience doesn't absolve a leader of his responsibility to do the right thing.*

6

After Operations Reconnaissance

THE AFTER OPERATIONS RECONNAISSANCE WAS a technique developed early and used often. A week after Operation HIT SQUAD Task Force Bear sent a patrol back to the objective, returning ID cards to the women, answering questions and ascertaining the impact of the previous operation. Their source had told them there were still weapons hidden underground outside the main residence next to a solitary tree.

The Battalion leadership was skeptical about the sources information. After all, the unit had already conducted a detailed search of the area, but since they were going to the objective anyway they decided it wouldn't hurt to do a little looking around. The reconnaissance took place during daylight, no doors were kicked in, no Iraqis were flex-cuffed or hooded, a cordon was not set. The four HMMWV patrol simply parked in a loose coil, established security, dismounted and knocked on the door to the courtyard of the main residence.

Bear 3 approached the old woman, who came to the door with her grandson. Her ID cards were returned. She asked about the men that were still in U.S. custody and when they would return. Bear 3 asked if there were any weapons left in the house or on the property. She assured him there were not. After a few more minutes of conversation using an interpreter, she was again asked if there were any additional weapons hidden somewhere on the property, to which the Iraqi matriarch answered “la” or no. Bear 3 told her he would take a quick look around the property and then walked the fifteen paces to the lone tree in the front yard. There was a cow tied off to it with hay spread around the base for the cow and other animals to feed off of. Bear 3 and a couple of soldiers shuffled through the hay and within thirty seconds had tripped upon a piece of wood. The wood, about the size of a half sheet of plywood, covered a hole containing a fifty-five gallon drum, empty except for the nine AK 47s and ammunition, wrapped and well oiled on the bottom.

The woman and her son or grandson were confronted, but provided no information. She claimed that she didn’t know how AK 47s and ammunition came to be buried in a fifty-five gallon drum just fifteen paces from her front door, or how the rest of the miscellaneous military equipment that was subsequently uncovered came to be on her property. What became an ever increasingly frustrating trend was the apparent lack of contrition by the Iraqi population, even in light of overwhelming evidence.

While militarily insignificant as far as the amount of weapons and equipment that were found, the after operations reconnaissance of the HIT SQUAD objectives provided some valuable lessons to a battalion struggling with the realities of a budding insurgency. First, the search techniques used during the initial operation left a lot to be desired. The tendency early on was to focus on the inside of buildings. Livestock was rarely moved and piles of bricks, trash and other refuse were not routinely dismantled. Metal detectors quickly became a must have item and those soldiers adept at finding hidden cache’s were identified and used on the search teams. Second, the local population, women and children included, had no problem lying and/or denying what was almost universally considered by American soldiers to be damning and convincing evidence.

This was immensely frustrating to anyone who routinely engaged the Iraqis as they could seemingly contradict themselves within minutes without batting an eye. The stories are simply too many to relate, but certainly many hours were lost to circular, deliberately vague and maddening conversations. Third, just because an objective has been cleared doesn't mean that it *is* clear. Finally, the mission confirmed the source as having accurate and timely information; i.e. he could be trusted.

Leadership Lessons

- *Revisit old objectives to assess the impact of your operations, determine the second and third order effects, and perhaps learn there are still targets that need to be addressed.*
- *Understanding of foreign cultures is a must-not just how to be polite or what kind of foods to expect but how specifically the foreign culture may affect what your organization is trying to accomplish, For example, it would have been helpful to understand that when an Iraqi lies, he or she is not dishonoring themselves or their family, they are protecting them; in other words in Iraqi culture a lie is expected if it furthers the cause of the family or benefits the group-this would have been useful information early in the conflict.*

7
Good Shoot/Bad Shoot

A LONG RANGE RECONNAISSANCE AND SURVEILLANCE (LRRS) team reported to Task Force Bear late one afternoon. The team had been sent by higher HQs as an expert force to establish an observation post (OP) at an emerging enemy engagement area. The site was an historic enemy ambush location where artillery shells rigged to detonate (later known as IEDs or improvised explosive devices) had twice exploded on the Bear Battalion Commander, Bear 6, in an attempt to assassinate him as he traveled to a scheduled meeting with local Sheiks. This was certainly a mission that the soldiers of the Battalion could have handled themselves, they hadn't asked for the help, but there is an old military adage of never turning away additional combat power. The fact is, the Battalion wasn't given the choice. The Brigade was sufficiently concerned by the assassination attempts against one of its Battalion Commanders that it sent in one of the few combat multipliers it had at its disposal.

The LRRS team arrived ready for a fight. They had all the latest kit and adhered to no particular uniform. It was obvious from their demeanor they felt they were a special unit. When asked if they had any equipment shortages or concerns prior to the mission, one of the non commissioned officers responded "don't worry sir, we've got enough firepower to handle anything that gets in the way." These were ominous words from a team whose forte was supposedly "reconnaissance and surveillance".

The plan was simple. The team would walk in from a drop off point and set up an observation post and security element, hopefully without being detected by the locals. The belief was that the enemy was setting in the IEDs at night because these were complex weapons that took time to emplace. The last IED consisted of five 152 mm rounds wired together with two of the rounds on a fifteen-minute delayed timer. This was considered pretty advanced at this stage of the conflict and an indication that the enemy in the area was well trained. Because there was so much civilian and military traffic during the day, the reasoning was that the IEDs were getting placed in at night. While patrols were being conducted, there was not enough combat power to provide a constant presence, leaving large time gaps, which allowed the enemy to do his work.

The insertion went flawlessly. The OP and security was established, and a tank platoon acting as the QRF waited at REDCON 1.5 sitting about ten kilometers away at Patrol Base Animal. The LRRS team reported over the radio as vehicular and pedestrian traffic moved through the area with nothing unusual occurring. After a few hours of trepidation, everyone relaxed. No one really expected contact on the first night of the operation, and there was no Sheik meeting the next day to confirm the pattern of attack on Bear 6. If contact was made or suspicious activity observed, the QRF would be notified and respond immediately. Rules of engagement allowed use of deadly force to protect life or property, with a positive identification and hostile intent or threat exhibited by the enemy.

At some point after 0100 the Battle Captain woke up Bear 3 with a report that there were two men walking past the OP with weapons and satchel charges. Less than a minute later the LRRS reported heavy small arms contact from the men in the road and from the surrounding area. The QRF had been eves dropping on the net and launched as soon as it heard the first contact report. Confusing reports of continued enemy small arms fire came in until the QRF arrived on the scene. The results, one enemy killed with another wounded. The wounded Iraqi had escaped into the nearby underbrush and date palm trees. A search was ongoing.

As soon as his HMMWV crew was ready, Bear 3 began his move to the site from the Battalion TOC located over 35km away. While moving the radio crackled with more contact. A dump truck had tried to run through the blocking position established by the QRF. The truck was disabled with several rounds shot into the engine compartment, another Iraqi dead and one wounded. The A Troop commander at Patrol Base Animal quickly stood up the secondary QRF and moved to evacuate the wounded Iraqi in the M113 military ambulance.

Bear 3 arrived at the scene as the first light of morning approached. The dead Iraqi lay in the road next to the satchel charge and an AK 47. A blood trail led off into the tall reeds on the North side of the road, where the second Iraqi had escaped. The large dump truck was still dripping fluid sat on the South side of the road. Something didn't feel right. There was a palpable sense of uneasiness. The LRRS patrol leader explained that the Iraqis had raised their AK 47s as his soldiers approached to detain them. Observing hostile intent his soldiers fired first. Small arms fire then erupted from different points along the road signaling to the team some kind of enemy ambush. Exchanges of gunfire lasted several minutes. After the firing subsided the dump truck drove through the blocking position. The LRRS team had disabled the truck with a burst of fire into the engine compartment. Several rounds were then fired into the cab as the two Iraqis inside resisted being pulled out. One reportedly had reached for a pistol.

The QRF platoon leader arriving from Patrol Base Animal within minutes of first contact told a slightly different story. When the QRF arrived the LRRS patrol leader had asked them to strafe several areas where enemy fire had come from. Checking his map, the QRF platoon leader realized he was being asked to fire on an area where one of the LRRS team's own security elements was supposed to be located. As they continued to deliberate on what actions to take, the LRRS security element in question walked onto the road from precisely the area they had just been discussing (the same one the LRRS platoon leader had wanted strafed by the tank). The dump truck had then run the blocking position, but the QRF platoon leader explained that his tanks had been parked with their headlights off. By the time they tried to signal the truck, it was too late for it to stop. The LRRS team had then opened fire on the truck, disabling it and then fired again into the cab while extracting the driver and passenger.

Bear 3 asked what was in the satchel charge. The LRRS patrol leader pointed to it, but recommended against picking it up. Something definitely didn't feel right. Bear 3 walked over to the bag, picked it up, no wires hanging from it, not too heavy. He dumped out the contents: fish. It was a bag of fish. The Iraqis had been fishing, or more likely stealing fish from a nearby fish farm.

The soldiers who had done the shooting bagged the body. Bear 3 loaded the body bag into the rear seat of his HMMWV and drove back to the task force headquarters.

Was it a good shoot? According to the information available, it was. The unwritten rule gives the benefit of the doubt to the soldier. The shooting of the Iraqis in the cab of the truck was murkier, but again, the benefit of the doubt must go to the soldier. The LRRS Team members and leaders clearly thought they were in danger when they opened fire and leaders must resist the temptation to remove the decision to shoot (or not shoot) from their soldiers. Every soldier in the U.S. Army is taught that they have an inherent right to protect themselves and others with lethal force if necessary.

But things could have been different. If there had been

an interpreter on the scene or the soldiers had known some simple Arabic phrases, the Iraqis may not have been as startled by armed men emerging from the darkness in the middle of the night. If the tanks had kept their lights on, or had reflectors or soldiers had placed a flashlight or chem-lights on the road ahead of the blocking position, the dump truck probably wouldn't have crashed through. Again, interpreters or a better understanding of the language would have allowed the soldiers to shout instructions to the men in the cab instead of trying to pull them out as a first option. Finally, it took months for some U.S. soldiers to realize that at night in Iraq it was normal for Iraqis to be carrying AK 47s for their own protection and is an ingrained part of their culture.

With all that said, there still was a feeling of uneasiness about the professionalism of the LRRS team. They just didn't come across as a disciplined unit, more of an ad hoc organization that was looking for a fight. The concerns were enough that the Battalion requested to Brigade that the LRRS not be used in their area for future operations. Unfortunately this wasn't the last shooting incident involving the LRRS.

A couple of weeks later the LRRS were inserted into TF Bear's area to establish observation of a suspected Al Qaeda-Iraq (AQI) sanctuary consisting of a number of houses and out buildings. Without consulting the Battalion or coordinating intelligence the LRRS team was inserted at night by helicopter. Within twenty minutes the LRRS team was compromised, had killed an Iraqi farmer and was extracted. Now the Bear Battalion was ordered to conduct a short notice raid on the suspected AQI houses and later to pay restitution to the family of the dead Iraqi. Of course the insertion, shooting and extraction of the LRRS team alerted any AQI that may have been in the area, so the short notice raid found nothing. The story from the family of the dead Iraqi farmer was that their father had seen men moving through his property, and fearing thieves went outside to scare them off. The LRRS team seeing an Iraqi with an AK 47 and fearing an ambush assumed he must be a terrorist and shot him.

Several weeks after this second event, the LRRS team was inserted again. This time to establish an OP observing historic indirect fire points of origin (POOs) to prevent mortars and rockets from being fired onto LSA Anaconda. Again, the team was compromised and again they killed an Iraqi farmer who was out in his fields at night with an AK 47.

So in three visits to AO Bear the LRRS team killed four Iraqis and wounded two; compromising their mission each time. In each case the soldiers involved got the benefit of the doubt And since they weren't attached or even OPCON to TF Bear, no formal investigation was conducted. This early in the war investigations of civilian deaths were not routinely done. The Brigade finally did move the LRRS team to focus on another area, but unfortunately they were again involved in a questionable shooting, this time with several more Iraqis killed. The team was ultimately recalled and left the Brigade's battlespace for good. It is unknown what became of them.

Unfortunately, civilian deaths at the hands of U.S. soldiers were not anomalies in Iraq. There are many reasons for this, but mostly it was due to lack of training and leadership. Early in the war most soldiers and leaders were not trained in local Iraqi patterns of life, customs or language. Military exercises prior to 2003 rarely if ever included civilians on the battlefield as significant parts of the training. After 2003 Army units getting ready to deploy adapted their home station training to better replicate the environment in Iraq. Arabic speakers were hired to act as role players during training exercises and cultural and language education became a priority. Soldiers were immersed in training environments that replicated the sights, sounds and complexities of the Iraqi battlefield. Replicating battlefield conditions is not a new concept in the Army, but prior to 2003 there had been little recognition that civilians on the battlefield would become such an important part of the tactical problem.

From a leadership perspective the issue was more complex. Army leaders at all levels are taught from day one that they have two priorities: to accomplish the mission and to take care of their soldiers. These two priorities present U.S. Army leaders with an enigma, because to accomplish any mission in Iraq requires leaders to send soldiers on operations that inherently place them at risk of death or serious injury. This enigma resulted in leaders sometimes making decisions that in the short term seemed like the right thing to do in order to take care of their soldiers, but in the long term may have contributed to a deterioration in the overall situation and detracted from overall mission accomplishment. Typical decisions included how quickly and when to escalate to the use of lethal force (e.g. when to open fire after a patrol was attacked with an IED); how to question and treat detainees (most of whom would eventually return to their communities and spread the word on how they were treated); or how aggressive to be with civilians during raids or other missions.

None of these situations has a clear black and white answer, but in general Army leaders tended to be more likely to respond with lethal force (i.e. would shoot their weapons) and be more physical with civilians early in the war. As the conflict progressed and leaders with multiple tours became more comfortable operating in the environment, they and their units were better able to discern when aggressive action or use of lethal force was appropriate.

As an organization the Army faces a dilemma in how they train their leaders for future conflicts. In a high intensity, traditional battle the Army's leaders want their soldiers and units to be aggressive and fire first. Any hesitation can result in an immediate catastrophic loss, for example in a tank on tank engagement. Most of the Army's shooting tables correctly reward the shooter for quick, accurate fire. The challenge is how to balance this absolute requirement for aggressive shooting with an appreciation for the second and third order consequences of weapons' effects that inadvertently injure or kill civilians. This type of training has become common throughout the Army today as units continue to rotate to places like Iraq and Afghanistan. The challenge is how to incorporate these lessons into the high intensity conflict (HIC) training, which the Army must eventually return to.

None of this discussion should discount the incredible pressure soldiers and leaders were under each time they went on patrol in Iraq. Being shot at makes you very willing to shoot back. Getting repeatedly targeted with IEDs, mortars and rockets and watching your peers get killed and maimed when you have no real enemy to face makes you *want* to shoot at something; makes you look forward to shooting at anything. Shooting a weapon in and of itself can be very therapeutic, even more so when you can shoot at an enemy that is attacking you.

One of the challenges in Iraq is that soldiers have very few legitimate chances to do just that, and this leads to frustration, despair and depression. Frustration, despair and depression of course lead soldiers to suicide, substance abuse and occasionally to make decisions that get civilians killed. That there haven't been more of these incidents in Iraq is a testament to the quality of leadership in the American Army, especially in the squads, platoons and companies where the war is being fought.

There is another frustration being born mostly by conventional units. Namely that when an outside agency and other "special" units conduct missions (the LRRS is not officially considered part of the special operations community, but in many cases falls outside the traditional leadership and supervisory channels) they are disproportionally more likely to inflict civilian casualties. There are few maneuver battalion commanders or operations officers from the first four years of the war who didn't have to make amends after outside units killed an Iraqi civilian during an operation. Normally the battle space owner would have only cursory knowledge of the outside unit's mission and would not be the beneficiary of any intelligence gained. But they would invariably be the one who had to pay restitution and sit with the Sheiks and Iraqi family members to explain why their relatives were killed. This was easily justifiable when the civilians were caught associating with terrorists, but too often this wasn't the case. There were certainly "A teams", numbered task forces and others that proved the exception to this rule, and by 2007 coordination between SOF and conventional forces had immensely improved, but too often there was some very real disruption of effort caused by competing missions, priorities and application of the ROE.

The fix for all of this, as alluded to above, is training and leadership. SOF organizations, or any other unit that falls outside a normal Brigade Combat Team construct, must be incorporated into brigade and battalion collective training events. Unity of command (and thereby unity of effort) must be demanded from all levels before deployment. The unity of command/effort problem was largely addressed as the war progressed, but even as late as 2009 outside units and agencies were still conducting operations that were desynchronizing and destabilizing the desired effects of the conventional battlespace owners.

This is not to diminish the tremendous work of the special operations community. They killed a lot of terrorists and insurgents that needed to die. They captured many who would otherwise have continued to attack U.S. soldiers and Iraqi civilians. But if conventional and SOF are going to operate in the same battlespace, and this seems likely on every imagined future battlefield, they must be better incorporated into pre-deployment training and must enhance unity of command and unity of effort instead of detracting from it.

Leadership Lessons

- *Beware the "experts". Don't assume outside agencies share your common vision or operating procedures. Just because they are supposed "experts" doesn't mean they will contribute to the success of your organization or the accomplishment of your goals. Take the time to understand their training level and goals before providing them the opportunity to desynchronize your efforts.*
- *Understand that the conditions your organization trained for may not be the same conditions it finds itself competing in; early recognition followed by retraining to the lowest level of leader is essential to mitigate unintended consequences and increase the chances for success.*

8

Tarmiyah Police Station

IN SEPTEMBER 2003 INSURGENTS OVERRAN THE TARMIYAH police station for the first time. The recently completed improvements and upgrades to the station, paid for by the U.S. government, including vehicles and weapons, were destroyed or stolen. All of the criminals and suspected insurgents held in the jail were released. To a man, the Iraqi police and members of the newly created Iraqi Civil Defense Corps (ICDC) who were guarding the police station fled without firing a shot or putting up any resistance; many of them peeling off their uniforms as they ran. The new Chief of Police, recently installed by Task Force Bear, watched the attack from across the street and took no action. Worse, he had predicted the attack would take place and had warned American forces of the threat just hours earlier, but had taken no other action to defend his station.

Shortly after the attack Task Force Bear occupied the police station with two infantry platoons, about seventy soldiers and officers, who fortified the station and remained in the center of the Iraqi town for six weeks. This began a pattern of insurgent attack, followed by American intervention, followed by American withdrawal, followed by insurgent attack that lasted into 2008. The later years of the battle for Tarmiyah have been documented in numerous articles. This is how it started.

Tarmiyah is a relatively rural area just north of Baghdad along the Tigris River. The town itself measures only three to five square kilometers, but Tarmiyah County, or "Qadah" in Arabic, measures many hundreds of square kilometers. It was affectionately dubbed the Iraqi Riviera because of its high priced homes and villas that abut the river. An almost exclusively Sunni area, it was historically used as a favorite bedroom community for general officers and other Baathist officials seeking to escape the heat of Baghdad summers. While the U.S. military was drawn to focus mostly on the town of Tarmiyah proper, the real power brokers, insurgent support zones and safe areas proved to be outside the town. Besides being mostly rural, Tarmiyah is also isolated. There is only one main road in and out, and even the few secondary roads can be easily blocked, observed or booby-trapped. The nearest U.S. presence at the time was patrol base Animal, approximately twenty kilometers away, which housed a company team from TF Bear.

Team Apache's primary task was security of MSR Tampa, the major supply route for all Coalition Forces in Iraq. Their priority was certainly not the town of Tarmiyah. The Task Force Bear headquarters was over forty kilometers away by paved road, thirty-five kilometers along a secondary road.

When Task Force Bear began conducting assessments and engagements with the Sheiks and local leadership of Tarmiyah in July 2003, there was little to no support for the newly arrived Americans. In fact Bear 6, was personally targeted for assassination on numerous occasions while driving to or from scheduled meetings with local Iraqi leaders. This included attacks using some very complex IEDs as early as July, before they had become a widespread threat throughout the country.

The attacks persisted despite daily interaction with the Iraqi population and civil leaders and the best efforts of

Task Force Bear's civil affairs team. Ongoing civil affairs projects focused on improving water distribution, education and medical care. Sheik councils and a functioning town council and mayor were elected or appointed. The local Sheiks' even pledged to control the violence against Coalition Forces in their area but attacks continued.

In an attempt to help control the area and involve the Iraqis in their own security, Task Force Bear turned to the Iraqi police for help. As everywhere else in Iraq however the hope that the Iraqi police would be able to secure the area or at least provide needed intelligence on insurgent and criminal activity was fruitless. Indeed in the nine months TF Bear spent in the Tarmiyah area, not one government employee, Sheik or prominent citizen willingly provided any information or material assistance to the Americans. Many covertly opposed them. The only significant person to come forward to provide any help was Abbas, the man eventually installed as the police chief, the one who watched passively from across the street as his district police station was overrun.

In July of 2003, Abbas approached TF Bear with information regarding the Baath hierarchy in the Tarmiyah and Mushaeda areas. He provided lists of names and an organizational structure to the TF intelligence officer, Bear 2. While only a single source, which is normally not enough corroboration to allow the information to be considered actionable, Abbas appeared trustworthy. A former police captain with Kurdish lineage, he was ousted from the police force by the Baathist regime and denied his pension or any benefits. It was his information that led the Task Force to conduct operation HIT SQUAD. It also provided the basis of understanding for the political and social networks in the Tarmiyah area. The veracity of the information he provided, while initially met with skepticism, was repeatedly confirmed either through operations or other Iraqi sources.

When Task Force Bear first entered Tarmiya the police

force was inept at best. Emulating police forces throughout Iraq, the police in Tarmiyah were content with staying at their station until after a crime was committed and/or they received an order from an investigating judge to conduct an inquiry. There was no tradition of community policing or active patrolling and the police force took no demonstrable action to curb the growing number of IEDs taking place in its area. As Task Force Bear leadership became increasingly frustrated by the lack of cooperation from the existing Chief of Police, they actively started to discuss targeting him for replacement. The most obvious choice for replacement, and really the only option considered, was Abbas. Not only was he a former police officer with anti Baathist sentiments, but he was also Coalition friendly and had already provided important information about the local area. He also adamantly declared his desire for the job claiming he would crush the insurgency within days of being appointed. He believed all that the people of Tarmiyah needed was a leader with an iron fist to keep them under control. Several times he implored the Americans to be more heavy-handed, at one point declaring that the only effective means of dealing with Iraqis was with "the whip". He also favored using beatings to extract information from those detained-and this was one of the good guys.

On the day the police station was overrun, Abbas had come to Forward Operating Base Bear with information that there would be a pro-Baathist demonstration in Tarmiyah that evening. The demonstration, he explained, was part of a plan by local insurgents to attack the police station using the cover of the protest to get in close. During the past week there had been a couple of other demonstrations in the general area. None had turned violent.

The Task Force Bear leadership didn't discount the threat, but believed their new police chief was up to the task of defending his station. Not only were they bolstered by the Chief's emphatic denunciation of the insurgents, but the police force had also recently received new weapons, vehicles and an infusion of the first graduating class of the Iraqi Civil Defense Corps (ICDC). (The ICDC was a security force hired and trained by Coalition Forces that became the precursor to the Iraqi National Guard Battalions and later to the Iraqi Army; see chapter 12) This was an opportunity for the fledging ICDC and the new Chief of Police to demonstrate their resolve, if not their proficiency.

To support Abbas the Task Force stationed a tank platoon as a ground QRF just five kilometers to the west and coordinated for AH64 Apache helicopters to overwatch the demonstration from just outside the town. It was decided to avoid an overt U.S. presence on the streets of Tarmiyah in an attempt to prevent U.S. forces from becoming the object of the demonstration and perhaps even inciting violence. Abbas, for his part, was vehemently opposed to this plan. He wanted a strong and plainly visible U.S. presence. Bear 6 and Bear 3 believed it was time for Abbas to start living up to his bluster about confronting the insurgents. With a team of Apache helicopters hovering a short distance outside the town and the ground QRF close by the TF Bear leadership was confident any planned attack would be deterred. Abbas left with the encouragement of the U.S. leadership and their belief that Abbas would go to the police headquarters in order to prepare for its defense.

A few hours later, as dusk approached, with the QRF set in position and the helicopters in overwatch, the first SPOTREPs started coming in over the radio. There were several hundred demonstrators with banners proclaiming their fealty to Saadam Hussein, urging his return. The procession moved down the main street of Tarmiyah under observation of the two Apaches. A few men with megaphones led the demonstrators in cheers and chants. As daylight faded, the demonstrators broke up. Needing to return to base for fuel and to avoid being caught in the transition period between daylight and darkness, when helicopters are particularly vulnerable, the flight of Apaches departed. Then the QRF was ordered to stand down. The last report was of the demonstrators being mostly dispersed, with no violence noted and the police station intact.

Within fifteen minutes, a UAV arrived overhead to resume overwatch of the town. The UAV operators reported seeing fires burning at the police station and individuals running in and out uncontested. Unfortunately, the military grid coordinate used to report the location of the event was inaccurate, leading the task force to delay its response as it attempted to confirm the information it was receiving. Regardless, it was too late. The police station had been overrun.

Abbas arrived at FOB Bear within the hour distraught and angry; distraught at the destruction of his station and angry that the Americans had not acted to prevent the attack. For his part, instead of going to the police station to warn his officers and make a stand, Abbas had positioned himself across the street to observe the demonstration. He took no action to intervene when locals swarmed the station. The insurgents had patiently waited for the Apache helicopters to depart before acting and took the station without firing a shot; with the police and ICDC discarding their uniforms before jumping the walls to escape. For their part, Bear 6 and Bear 3 couldn't understand how Abbas, who had done nothing but proclaim his willingness to confront the local insurgents, had passively stood and watched as the station was overrun.

The results: all of the Iraqi Police vehicles were destroyed or stolen, all furniture, communications equipment and weapons stolen or destroyed, structural damage and fire to the buildings, all criminals released. More importantly, the Tarmiyah police, their new Chief and the ICDC were all discredited in the eyes of the population.

It is more difficult to assess the impact of the non-intervention by U.S. forces. On the face of it, Task Force Bear could easily have prevented the takeover of the police headquarters by positioning troops at the station or along the route of the protest. What is not known is what other problems would have resulted from an aggressive U.S. stance. Would U.S. forces have been attacked, perhaps being drawn into an overreaction causing extensive civilian casualties? What would the impact of that type of situation have had on the Iraqi population? Would it have galvanized the burgeoning resistance? It is impossible to know.

The subsequent response from Task Force Bear was swift. Before midnight the police station was occupied by most of a U.S. infantry company. Roads inside the city were barricaded and closed. In the effort to improve the defenses of the station and move heavy Bradley Fighting Vehicles into the town, curbstones were ripped up and the center of town was turned into a fortified bastion. The energy and diligence of the American soldiers at their task was inspiring. Soon, crew served weapons bristled from rooftops and warning shots ripped through the downtown area to send a message to the locals not to try any further attacks.

With the American soldiers in place the Iraqi Police and ICDC started trickling back to work over the next week. The ICDC proved the easiest to entice and hold to task; mostly because they were being paid directly by the U.S. Army. The police too finally returned, largely to ensure they continued to receive they're pay, which had been increased substantially by the Coalition Provisional Authority. It is important to comment that they did not return because they were particularly incensed at the recent attack and were now ready to work with Task Force Bear. None of the police or ICDC, with the exception of Chief Abbas, ever provided information on who may have conducted the attack. They returned only to receive a paycheck in a country where a steady paying government job was a prized and coveted possession. The fact that the

Iraqi Security Forces did return provided at least a modicum of hope for the soldiers, NCOs and Officers of Task Force Bear, who now had to figure out how to secure and resupply this isolated outpost in the middle of a hostile country.

Despite its drawbacks, there were several benefits to being in downtown Tarmiyah. It provided a twenty-four hour presence of U.S. Forces, which in theory should at least dissuade open fighting or coercion of the population and Iraqi Security Forces. It provided easier access for Iraqis who were willing to provide information to Americans on the budding insurgency and/or criminal activity in the area. It provided an inherent partnership with the IP and ICDC to conduct patrols and force protection. It provided a secure meeting place for the leadership of TF Bear to engage with the Chief of Police and other town leaders. It also provided daily contact with the Iraqi people and gave them a chance to see that American soldiers were not the boogey men some portrayed them as.

Unfortunately, the first occupation of Tarmiyah also presented a number of tactical problems for Task Force Bear. Although it controlled the police station and the immediate downtown area, the Task Force could not project combat power into the countryside because of all the specified and implied tasks that needed to be accomplished. Towers and gates at the police station required manning twenty-four hours a day, seven days a week. Soldiers and leaders were needed to staff the command post and monitor the radios. Joint and independent patrols were conducted and a QRF on as little as five-minute recall was always on standby. Other tasks such as supply operations, maintenance of vehicles and the need for continuous force protection improvements (building bunkers, sandbagging windows etc…) meant that those soldiers manning the police station had a full time job just surviving. A situation euphemistically referred to as a "self licking ice cream cone".

The remaining platoons in the Task Force were fully engaged in other tasks and couldn't be spared to assist. Those tasks included Task Force Bear's essential task of disrupting IED cells influencing MSR TAMPA, defending and supporting two additional patrol bases, providing two additional area QRFs, counter-mortar/counter-rocket tasks associated with the defense of Forward Operating Base Anaconda, and a platoon devoted to training the ICDC. In addition there were enduring detainee operations (there were few days when the battalion didn't have someone detained at the FOB), a daily effort to remove the tens of thousands of rounds of ammunition littering the battlespace, engagements and meetings with local leaders and ongoing Civil Affairs projects that had to be scouted and checked. All of these tasks competed for the short supply of troops and prevented Task Force Bear from dominating the terrain surrounding Tarmiyah.

Without a force that could continuously influence the area two to ten kilometers around the police station, the enemy could maintain freedom of maneuver and initiative to launch coordinated mortar, RPG, small arms and IED attacks. With the Battalion HQ over a forty-five minute ground movement away, requiring navigation through several enemy engagement areas, it was clearly not in an ideal location to influence the fight in Tarmiyah. Although a recommendation to move the TF HQ and build a patrol base closer to Tarmiyah was discussed, the myriad of competing and higher priority tasks won out. The result was a Battalion Task Force that that had exhausted its available manpower, but was not in a position to decisively conclude any of its tasks. This "troops to task" problem was not unique to Task Force Bear in the fall of 2003. The lack of adequate combat power meant that leaders routinely had to put off or curtail operations that needed doing. Despite assurances at the time from various senior leaders that no more troops were needed in Iraq, most battalion task forces could easily have absorbed another company or two and still had too much to do.

The impact the attack against the police station had on the local Iraqi population was also significant. The success of the insurgents to easily overpower and intimidate both the Iraqi Police and ICDC sent a clear signal that they were not ready to protect the population. In fact, the recent improvements in the police force, new Chief of Police, new vehicles, new weapons and uniforms, coupled with the introduction of the ICDC into downtown Tarmiyah most likely precipitated the attack. In this way the insurgents disparaged the newly formed Iraqi Security Forces just as they were beginning to show progress and become more visible and successful in the community. Equally important, the insurgents showed that U.S. Forces could or would not protect them. While the subsequent and immediate occupation of the police station by American soldiers clearly showed resolve, it also put the Iraqis who lived in and around the downtown area at risk and completely disrupted the town's normal atmosphere. Local Iraqis actually felt less safe as attacks against American forces living at the police station sometimes resulted in killed or injured Iraqi civilians. Within days the town leadership was asking Bear 6 to remove his American soldiers from the town.

Over the next six weeks U.S. troops living at the Tarmiya police station were attacked regularly every four to five days. If the occupation had lasted longer, it is difficult to imagine that the attacks wouldn't have gotten more severe and better coordinated as they did during subsequent years and occupations; finally resulting in an S-VBIED and complex attack that killed two and wounded twenty-seven of the thirty-five U.S. soldiers defending the station in 2007. Despite the casualties, the station was not overrun.

The reason American Forces finally departed the police station in 2003 was not because of any belief that the area had been pacified or that the ISF had improved sufficiently to secure the city. Instead, in what was an obvious sign that there were too few troops to accomplish all of the specified and implied tasks, they were pulled to augment another mission. The troops were needed to provide a reserve force for the U.S. operation to retake the city of Samara, to the North, from control of insurgents. This mission was to last three days. Instead the mission lasted over three months and Task Force Bear saw its combat power reduced permanently by thirty-three percent.

Leadership Lessons

- *Sometimes there is no "right" solution to a problem. The most difficult decisions to make are those that aren't defined in black and white; the so-called "grey" area. Few are comfortable operating in the grey area, fewer still are good at it and only the exceptional have the understanding and judgment to flourish there.*
- *To figure out the best solution, second and third order consequences must be considered. (Was it right to keep U.S. forces out of the town and away from the demonstration the night the police station was attacked? Was it correct to hastily occupy the police station with a heavy U.S. presence at the expense of being able to conduct other operations and without a commitment to stay long term? What were the second and third order effects of the actions taken and what would the second and third order consequences have been if different actions had been taken?)*
- *Beware initial success; it may trigger an attack or action by your adversary to discredit your progress.*

9

Operation "SNATCH"/Interference from the Boss

ONE OF THE THIRD ORDER EFFECTS OF THE FIRST INSURgent attack on the Tarmiyah police station in September 2003 was that the Chief of Police became compelled to act. With the Americans entrenched at the station, Abbas delivered information implicating over a dozen Iraqis who were either directly involved in the attack or who were responsible for coordinating and directing the fledging insurgent activity. On his list were several individuals who had previously worked with Coalition Forces along with their relatives, including the sons of the de facto mayor of Tarmiyah Sa'ad Mohamed. Abbas promised that with U.S. support he would lead a small team of trusted Iraqi Police to capture the individuals on his list. In less than twenty-four hours, a plan was produced and troops were in place, ready to execute. The targeted individuals were divided between the U.S. and Iraqi forces. Locals, friends of Abbas who agreed to act as guides, were used to take the U.S. troops to the various target houses. Abbas captured others on the list himself. A forward command post and QRF were established on an old training base just west of the town. Bear 2 and other intelligence specialists were positioned forward in order to conduct tactical questioning and interrogation on site, instead of waiting for those captured to be moved to the rear. This helped screen people of interest from those who happened to be at the wrong place at the wrong time. The operation took most of a day to accomplish with simultaneous "cordon and search" or "soft raids" taking place throughout the area. Targets were prioritized to go after the most influential first.

These types of short notice missions became the norm for units all over Iraq. A small patrol, three or four unarmored or "slick" HMMWVs with ten to fourteen American soldiers, plus local interpreters and sources/informants, would move into a house or group of houses. The patrol established a cordon and then knocked on the front door. The occupants would be questioned and the premises searched. With so few soldiers on the ground, cordons were formed either by positioning HMMWVs to cover rear exits, or in tight urban areas, simply sending a pair of soldiers to the rear of the house. Often because most Iraqis, who were acting as informants, were completely incapable of locating an objective area on a map or sattelite imagery, exact locations were unknown, precluding the detailed planning usually conducted by military units. This forced platoons, companies and battalions to be flexible and aggressive, trading the precision and safety of a well planned operation for the tempo and initiative gained through quick, decisive action: junior leaders (captain, lieutenants, platoon sergeants and staff sergeants) making on the spot decisions on whether to pursue a lead or return to base; whether to go in hard by kicking down a door and/or driving a HMMWV or M3 through a gate or simply knocking and waiting for the residents to come to the door; whether to detain all military aged males on an objective or only the those on the target list; whether to spend the time on a detailed search or quickly move to the next objective before a warning could be sent.

Surprisingly, these operations were usually effective

and of relatively low risk. With hundreds of Iraqi homes entered and detainees taken, and operations conducted both day and night, going in soft and hard, no U.S. casualties were taken on an objective in the TF Bear area of operations. In fact, for Task Force Bear there weren't even any enemy shots fired entering an Iraqi house in over nine months of counterinsurgency operations. It has often been repeated that the safest place to be in Iraq was raiding an Iraqi house, hard, at 0200 hours in the morning. For most soldiers this type of operation was much preferred to the endless, mundane hours of counter-IED patrols where first contact was usually made when the IED detonated next to your vehicle. (Aside: In late 2006 and 2007, this threat situation changed significantly, especially in places like the city of Baqubah in the province of Diyala, Iraq, where insurgents, and specifically AQI, began booby trapping houses; often enticing U.S. soldiers to enter the house before detonating the explosives. This tactic resulted in significant U.S. deaths as reported in open source media.)

The other surprising aspect of these operations was how generally compliant and cooperative the locals were. While it was certainly true that questioning many Iraqis was a maddening exercise in futility (it often took hours just to get their names), it was also not unheard of for Iraqis to turn in or provide information about their relatives. Some Iraqi women, wives in particular, seemed fed up with their husband's activities and the danger they were bringing to their families. If shown respect and made to feel they wouldn't be assaulted, abused or robbed, Iraqi women often spoke frankly and openly, especially if there were no Iraqi males present.

A practice that became common when entering a home was to have the female head of the household accompany the searchers. She would be handed any cash or jewelry and identification cards found during the search to give her confidence the family wouldn't be left destitute. She was also afforded the opportunity to open locked doors or cabinets instead of having soldiers break them open. Using this technique also afforded some practical security advantages. Having an Iraqi female lead you through a home provided an instant barometer of whether potential threats existed behind the next door or in the next room. Her facial expressions and body language would indicate proximity to a threat. Her refusal to enter a certain room or open a container would suggest to the searchers that they needed to proceed with caution.

There were of course examples of females who were not as compliant. One who locked herself in her bathroom, crying hysterically, terrified that her husband would find out that she had been alone with Americans in her house, thus making her unclean and potentially marked for death. Another who refused to answer even mundane questions about her name even after her ID cards were found and who was aggressive in ordering the TF Bear soldiers out of the house, refusing water and other offers of aid for her children. Lastly, there was the time a group of Iraqi women hid a targeted individual by sitting on him and covering him with their burqahs. These types of incidents were the exception. As Task Force Bear gained a reputation for treating the population fairly, there was less trepidation of allowing U.S. soldiers into Iraqi houses. In fact, generally speaking, Iraqis came to prefer U.S. soldiers to Iraqi Police, and later, to the Iraqi Army, entering their houses. They were more assured of fair treatment and less likely to be abused or robbed.

The net result of operation BEAR SNATCH was several low level detentions and one particularly prominent sheik in captivity. The Chief of Police had been true to his word, personally rounding up suspects and assisting U.S. forces at every turn. The leaders of Task Force Bear and the Iraqi police congratulated each other on mission accomplishment and began the arduous process of questioning and sorting through the detainees. Going to bed that night there was much optimism that the corner had been turned in Tarmiyah, that the right people had been detained and the information gained from their questioning would lead to further operations and success. The fact that the right people had been captured was confirmed by developments the next day.

Sometime around noon, the day after operation BEAR SNATCH, the Chief of Police and Tarmiyah Mayor Sa'ed Mohamed arrived at Forward Operating Base Bear. It was immediately apparent through body language, inflection and the passion of their requests, that something was wrong. Chief Abbas and the mayor took turns emphatically arguing for the release of Sheik Sadoon, the most important capture from the previous day's operation. While this was not too surprising to hear from Mayor Mohamed, whose own sons were implicated in the attack on the Tarmiyah police station and who had generated a fair share of suspicion on his own, the fact that Chief of Police Abbas was reversing himself on such an important capture was incomprehensible. Just the night before he had assured Bear 6 and Bear 3 that Sheik Sadoon was the most important and influential sheik in Tarmiyah; the man behind the curtain directing the anti Coalition Forces attacks. Now he was begging for his release. With Bear 6 out conducting battlefield circulation, Bear 3 and Bear 2 took Mayor Mohamed and the Chief to one of the old Iraqi ammunition bunkers on the FOB that had been converted to a questioning area. It was a dank, poorly lit room with a table and a few chairs. There were no windows or ventilation. Chief Abbas chose to wait outside, removing himself as a contributor; demonstrating his subordination to the mayor. This was unexpected as Abbas had previously been outspoken in his defiance of the insurgents and had never before held back in his criticism of those he felt responsible for the increasing violence.

Once inside, Mayor Mohamed quickly got to the point, demanding the release of Sheik Saddon. He argued that the Sheik was an old man, that he had nothing to do with the insurgency, that he was very influential in the local area and that he could help stop the attacks against Coalition Forces. Bear 2 and Bear 3 remained unconvinced and began a line of questioning in an attempt to find out what the connection between Mayor Mohamed and Sheik Sadoon really was and what information he could provide about the attack on the police station. The mayor's implication that he and Sheik Sadoon could help quell the violence in the area if Sadoon was released bolstered the belief that he knew more than he was telling. As the atmosphere in the bunker became more intense, with the air hazy from Mayor Mohamed's cigarettes, he finally blurted out, "If you don't release Sadoon then you must arrest me," adding, "I will not leave here without him." Bear 2 expertly used circular questioning to back him into a corner. Either he knew more than he was admitting, or he had no foundation to request the release of the Sheik.

While the questioning continued, Bear 3 went outside to check on Abbas. Considering him as close to a friend as there could be in 2003 between an American officer and an Iraqi, and perplexed by Abbas's apparent reversal, Bear 3 asked what had happened since the day before to make him change his mind. Immediately Abbas began to cry. Not proudly or reservedly, but despondently and openly. He stated, in a tear soaked voice, "You must help me. They will kill my family if you do not let Sadoon go." He would not explain who the people who had threatened him were. He would not explain himself further. "You must help me" was all he would say. Bear 3 surmised that for the reaction of Abbas to be so visceral, coupled with the mayor's willingness to be thrown into a Coalition prison before returning to Tarmiyah without Sadoon, it could only mean that they had detained the right guy.

As the questioning continued into mid-afternoon, Bear 2 and Bear 3 became more and more convinced they detained the right guy in Sheik Sadoon. They were also convinced that the mayor was at least complicit in the attack on the Tarmiyah police station and perhaps other insurgent activity as well. At the very least, he knew more than he was telling. Despite the potential implication to the Chief of Police and his family, Bear 2 and Bear 3 were ready to recommend to their boss, Bear 6, to keep Sadoon locked up. Additionally they were prepared to recommend to also arrest the mayor. They would figure out how to help protect Abbas's family later.

During a break in the questioning, Bear 3 and Bear 2 agreed on a course of action. When Bear 6 returned from his battlefield circulation they would recommend the mayor be detained for questioning. They had enough circumstantial evidence to warrant his detention if for no other reason than to be run up the chain and vetted. At least this would take him off the street for a number of months and perhaps precipitate a change in leadership in the Tarmiyah area. Before they could act on this recommendation the plan was thwarted from an unexpected source.

Shortly after Bear 3 and Bear 2 made this decision, Bear 6 returned. Unfortunately he arrived with an Army Senior Leader (Strike 6) in tow (Senior Leaders in the Army today include those in the rank of full Colonel (O6) and General Officers). This particular Senior Leader's area of responsibility included the Tarmiyah area. He had serendipitously been conducting his own battlefield circulation nearby and had decided to stop at FOB Bear for an assessment of the recent operations. Without discussing the results of the previous two plus hours of questioning or getting any additional background information, Strike 6 inserted himself into the negotiating/questioning process and took over the meeting. The results were disastrous with significant short term and long term implications.

Within thirty minutes, Strike 6 managed to undo all of the work of the previous two plus hours. In exchange for the mayor's pledge to support an anti violence resolution to be signed by local sheiks, Strike 6 agreed to release Sheik

Sadoon at once; not even keeping him detained long enough to be properly interrogated or questioned. He ordered Bear 3 to have Sadoon brought to the meeting room and delivered to mayor Mohamed for immediate release. Strike 6 then warned Mayor Mohamed that if violence in the area didn't abate, he would bring all the combat power at his disposal against the town of Tarmiyah. Convinced that he had made a substantial impression on the mayor the meeting concluded.

The history of the next five years is a testament to the results of this meeting. Not only did the violence not abate, but the Tarmiyah police station was overrun repeatedly. So much so that by 2007 the police had completely vacated the station and moved their headquarters to the nearby town of Mushahedah. Additionally, the route into Tarmiyah endured as an IED hotspot, wounding and killing American soldiers on numerous occasions. Sadly, as was subsequently proved in 2007, Sheik Sadoon *was* deeply imbedded in insurgent activity not only in Tarmiyah but throughout the country. Tarmiyah (the county as opposed to just the town) became known as a Sunni insurgent support zone and safe haven. The mayor was also implicated. Years later, finally tired of the killing which had cost him the lives of some of his own family members, Mayor Mohamed turned and became an open supporter of the Coalition.

For his part, Strike 6 was completely out of his element. He didn't realize when he sat down at the table across from Mayor Mohamed that he had entered a negotiation with an expert negotiator. He hadn't collected the background information he needed or consulted with Bear 2 or Bear 3 to determine what the desired outcome should be. He assumed that his rank and his intellect would carry the day against a less sophisticated and easily intimidated opponent. He proved wrong on both counts. Mohamed got everything he wanted, not least of which was the prestige from his countrymen for besting the Americans. The Sheiks of Tarmiyah never signed the security pact, at least not in 2003 or early 2004 and violence only increased. This lack of situational awareness repeated itself over and over again in Iraq during the next several years, leading to starts and stops, a choppy and hesitant strategy that failed to consider the application of effects over time.

Leadership Lessons

- *Every meeting is a negotiation; come prepared.*
- *Don't assume that rank/position or relative power will sway an opponent; both may be irrelevant to his desired outcome.*
- *When someone you have come to trust reverses themselves inexplicably, be confidant something nefarious in behind the change and take appropriate action.*

10

Tarmiyah Boundaries/Vision and Endstate

TASK FORCE BEAR'S DIFFICULTY GAINING CONTROL OVER Tarmiyah was duplicated by each subsequent unit responsible for the area through at least 2008. This was certainly not due to a lack of effort by the officers, non-commissioned officers and soldiers of the various battalions who spent whole years of their lives trying to solve this particular tactical problem. Money was spent, town councils and city governments were created, schools were built, Sheiks were consulted, local security forces were trained and equipped, local insurgents were captured and killed, public affairs messages extolling the benefits of the progress were distributed, yet the population continued supporting the insurgents and resisting the Coalition. The following are just a few examples of the continued violence in Tarmiyah during these subsequent years:

In February 2004 the Tarmiyah Chief of Police, Abbas, was gunned down along with two IP guards as he traveled home from work one evening. His car forced off the road and the bodies riddled with bullets from AK 47 fire.

In the spring of 2004, an IED or land mine detonated in a local soccer field that had recently been dedicated by U.S.

forces to the people of Tarmiyah. A number of children were injured in the attack. This deliberate targeting of Iraqi children was a warning to the population against accepting even seemingly benign gifts from the Americans.

In 2005 an IED detonated on a dismounted patrol killing three and wounding five U.S. soldiers.

In December 2006, the one hundred and fifty man Tarmiyah police force quit en masse and abandoned the police station. Manned only by a small U.S. contingent, the police station was completely destroyed a few months later (February 2007) by a S-VBIED and complex insurgent attack that killed two and wounded twenty-seven U.S. soldiers.

In April 2007, U.S. forces discovered that the recently completed Huda girl's school was rigged to explode with artillery rounds and propane tanks under the floors. It was a school paid for by U.S. forces and scheduled to open the following week. It is not clear if the intent was to detonate the bombs after the school was occupied, but the message was clear; don't take help from the Americans. The fact that the target was a girls' school should also be noted.

In August 2008, a suicide bomber killed one and wounded two U.S. soldiers and four civilians responding to an earlier IED attack. The attack was designed to target those first responding to the attack with an IED set with a delayed timer.

These are just a few examples of the types of attacks that persisted in Tarmiyah throughout the years of U.S. involvement. The fact that violence was so difficult to quell in such a relatively unimportant, sparsely populated, rural area serves as an example of how difficult a problem the Army faced throughout Iraq.

In what may prove analogous to other areas of the country, the persistence of the problem set in Tarmiyah may have been precipitated as much by form as it was by function. In other words, the form established by Coalition Forces (number of troops, location of troops and military boundaries) directly impacted the functionality (the ability to operate effectively) of the American units, Iraqi Security Forces, government infrastructure and Iraqi societal network.

Historically the Tarmiyah District or "Qadah" is part of Baghdad Province though it lies outside of the Baghdad city limits. To the North of Tarmiyah is Sa ala Din Province but the demarcation line between the Baghdad and Sa ala Din provinces is a question of some debate even among local Iraqis. It is not unusual for tribal affiliation to trump provincial boundaries, as tribal leaders will travel to the location most likely to garner their tribe the best advantages. Sometimes this means they will travel to different local governments, playing one against the other for support. In any case, it was generally accepted that the Tarmiyah Qadah boundary went as far north as the town("nahiyah" in Arabic) of Abayache, West past MSR Tampa and the town of Mushaeda and South to Taji, though the exact boundaries of these nahiyahs were also not clear. In fact the Tarmiyah District Chief of Police's contention was that his responsibility also included the police station and town of Saba Bor, which was a non-contiguous neighborhood clearly within the Baghdad city limits Southwest of Taji. Taji had been run as a military city under the previous Iraqi regime so had no civilian administrative infrastructure in place once the Iraqi military was disbanded.

Layered on top of this already confusing set of Iraqi boundaries was a competing set of Coalition Forces military boundaries. Task Force Bear was the southernmost battalion in the southernmost maneuver brigade from Multi National Division North (MND-N) based out of Tikrit, in Sa ala Din Province. Initially the Division Artillery Brigade was further south in Taji, but Task Force Bear assumed this battle space in late January 2004 as the DIVARTY redeployed to the United States. This made TF Bear the southernmost battalion in the MND-N footprint with well over 1,200 square kilometers of operating area. So most of Task Force Bear's battlespace ended up being in the Baghdad Qadah (Tarmiyah + Taji), but its higher HQ was based to the North in Sa ala Din. Because of this, the U.S. brigade and division, working with the Iraqis in Tikrit, the Sa ala Din provincial capital, were planning and coordinating and spending money on infrastructure and conducting military operations based on priorities developed for Sa ala Din Province. The Iraqi Sheiks and civilian leaders and people of Tarmiyah were not accounted for in these priorities because, as the Iraqi leaders in Tikrit properly pointed out, Tarmiyah was not part of their province; money and support and leadership for them would have to come from Baghdad.

The U.S. Division and Corps headquarters in Baghdad didn't have Tarmiyah on its radar screen, however, because Tarmiyah lay outside the Division and Corps boundary. They didn't have authority or the responsibility to plan or conduct operations in Tarmiyah. Additionally, when compared to the huge infrastructure, administrative and security problems encountered in Baghdad proper, Tarmiyah certainly seemed like an area where Coalition Forces could accept some risk. Even for the Task Force Bear leadership this problem of unaligned boundaries didn't become apparent for several months. The complexity of the Iraqi administrative and tribal system also contributed to the confusion. Additionally, with the exception of Chief of Police Abbas, no prominent Iraqi from the Tarmiyah area had offered Task Force Bear any help in understanding how the local government functioned. Just trying to determine who the existing government ministry representatives were took months. Many remained reticent or openly hostile toward working with Americans throughout OIF 1.

By November 2003 Task Force Bear had at least begun to figure out what some of the challenges surrounding this issue of boundaries and military/government support were.

With several challenges to resolve, including the hiring and firing of police officers and local government officials (Chief Abbas was still not officially recognized by the ministry in Baghdad and had not yet received any pay), Task Force Bear's leadership conducted a patrol to the Baghdad "Green Zone". With the exception of an unplanned detour into Sadr City, results were positive. The Baghdad HQs agreed to send a local Iraqi government expert who was contracted by the U.S. Government to assist with the development of the Tarmiyah Qadah Council and help link the Qadah to Baghdad's government and services. Additionally, as redeployment of various units loomed, thereby marking the transition from OIF 1 to OIF 2, the brigade and division headquarters supported the recommendation to realign military boundaries with the pre-existing Iraqi boundaries. In theory this should have allowed follow on U.S. forces to better coordinate infrastructure and government service improvements with military civil affairs and security efforts. Unfortunately the execution of the boundary realignment did not fully meet this intent.

The military boundary change was planned to coincide with the redeployment and relief in place (RIP) of the various divisions, brigades and battalions moving into Baghdad and Sa ala Din provinces. What happened was less than ideal. The boundary change was scheduled to take place in early April coinciding with the divisional transfers of authority, but because subordinate brigades and battalions usually completed their transfers of authority before the division's, there developed a gap between when the arriving battalion headquarters would be ready to accept responsibility for the area (on or about 18 March) and when the boundary change would go into effect (around 1 April).

Task Force Bear began its RIP process in March 2003 with an inbound battalion that had already been told it would be moving to occupy different battlespace by early April. While the relief in place was thorough, there was understandable inertia from the staff and soldiers of the incoming unit who knew this would not be their permanent home or responsibility. The energy it takes to establish relationships with the local leaders, become immersed in the local threat and political situation and conduct an exhaustive reconnaissance of the terrain is prohibitive and impossible to achieve with any fidelity in a two-week period. In fact, lead elements of the follow on battalion, the one affiliated with the division in Baghdad, had already arrived and were looking to begin their own relief in place before all of Task Force Bear had departed. The result was two inadequate reliefs in place completed in less than four weeks in an area recognized as an insurgent support zone with historically poor tribal and government links.

Adding to the complexity of the situation was the fact that the new military boundary still did not conform to the Iraqi provincial boundary. Worse it actually split the Tarmiyah Qadah in half. The Army planners putting pen to acetate, or more likely snapping lines on PowerPoint, arbitrarily delineated the military boundary just north of the *town* of Tarmiyah instead of including the entire Qadah of Tarmiyah and its satellite neighborhoods. This was important because all of the most dangerous and influential insurgent controlled areas in the Tarmiyah Qada were outside of the town limits. The new military boundary ensured that these areas would remain safe zones for the insurgents for the next several years.

This is not to imply that the incoming unit ignored its responsibilities. Security and civil affairs operations continued and actually increased during several periods in the years to come, but with the unit responsible for Tarmiyah commuting from over twenty kilometers away in Taji, which had its own set of security issues, and with the most significant insurgent sanctuaries placed outside of the unit's area of responsibility through the design of a planner who had never walked the ground, it is not surprising that Coalition Forces efforts in Tarmiyah floundered.

In Army parlance, a "gap" was created. With the unit to the South, constrained by a boundary and unable to project enough combat power to dominate the terrain, and the unit to the North so far away, focused on areas like Ad Dujayl and Balad, the "form" created by the higher headquarters clearly inhibited the "function" of the soldiers and leaders on the ground. One of the third order effects created by this gap was that by 2006, the police station and town council in the nahiyah of Arbayache, one of the satellite towns North of Tarmyah, was completely shut down. Not only was there no Coalition Force presence, but also the semblance of Iraqi government and security infrastructure that was in place when Task Force Bear left in early 2004, had completely dissolved. The Abayache police station was closed and deserted.

How was this situation able to develop? There are several root causes beyond the reasons already stated. A key component was the lack of a clearly defined vision and endstate for U.S. units serving in Iraq after the Iraqi Army was destroyed and the government of Iraq displaced. As late as July 2003 all of the members of Task Force Bear, from the battalion commander to the private soldier, expected a return to the United States by September or Christmas at the latest. They all believed (and had been told) that the objectives of the war in Iraq had been met; "mission accomplished".

The reality was more convoluted. Once it was clear that the perceived WMD threat was nescient, development of a specific follow on military objective proved elusive. Was it as simple as capturing Saddam or was there some other objective? By November 2003 the Coalition Provisional Authority (CPA) announced that an Iraqi interim government would be established by June 2004, thereby shifting responsibility of governing the country from the Coalition to the Iraqis. But the conditions on the ground, especially the growing number of attacks against U.S. forces, the ICDC and police, not to mention against organizations like the United Nations and even Iraqi religious leaders, all belied serious problems. Without a defined endstate and clearly articulated vision for U.S. military forces, it was difficult for them to prioritize tasks and resources toward a common goal.

As an example, the growing number of insurgent attacks did not deter the U.S. Army from starting to redeploy much of its heavy armor in November 2003. By that time Task Force Bear had moved most of its M1 tanks to Kuwait. To make matters worse units deploying as part of OIF 2 in March and April of 2004, like the battalion that replaced Task Force Bear, did so with much of their heaviest weapons still sitting in motorpools stateside.

Clearly there was a failure to recognize the growing insurgency for what it was and a failure to present a vision for how the U.S. Army would counter that insurgency. A clear endstate also proved ephemeral as the goals of military operations shifted from defeating the Iraqi Army to finding WMD, to capturing Saddam and his high ranking henchmen, to standing up the Iraqi Civil Defense Corps, to turning over power to the Iraqi interim government. The problem of defining an endstate endured for much of the conflict and directly influenced the decisions leaders made about what types of troops and how many were needed, where to position them on the battlefield, what types of equipment were needed and what types of operations to conduct.

Because of the lack of a clearly communicated vision and definable endstate, there was subsequently no clear operational framework or campaign plan that linked effects over time. And because many higher echelon staffs were focused on leaving as opposed to focusing on how to defeat a growing insurgency there was no urgency to create a plan. In fact there was not even clear consensus that an insurgency existed. The term insurgency was unofficially banned from use in the U.S. Army to describe the ongoing conflict until sometime in 2004. How could a staff develop a counterinsurgency campaign plan when there was no agreement that an insurgency existed in the first place?

Contributing to this problem was the dearth of counterinsurgency experience on staffs at every level. While squad, platoon, company and battalion level leaders were quickly applying lessons learned on the ground in Iraq, the higher-level staffs were filled with officers without counterinsurgency experience and only a cursory counterinsurgency education at best. Counterinsurgency techniques and theories were not taught as part of military education before the Command and General Staff College level (about the twelfth year of military service) and then only as an elective. This resulted in what is arguably the most professional and educated officer corps in the world being without serious academic exposure to insurgencies, guerrilla warfare or methods to counter them. Staff officers at the highest levels, who were responsible for writing the operations orders, producing the plans and delineating military boundaries had no experiential or educational base to draw from.

This is no one's fault. It is merely a product of an Army previously focused exclusively on high intensity warfare. As a result, orders from higher headquarters normally defaulted to large "sweeps" against mostly urban areas involving large formations, projected from bases for relatively short periods of time. There were of course exceptions, especially at the battalion level and below. However, the conflict in Iraq could not be won exclusively by squads, platoons, companies and battalions, even though that's where most of the fighting was being done. Winning required an operational construct that addressed the broad cultural, political and religious issues facing the country, and this required vision with commensurate endstate.

Another result of the lack of vision early in the war was that the wrong metrics were used to judge progress and success. After it became clear that there were no WMD to be found, various measures of effectiveness were created to gauge progress. Number of attacks, number of IEDs, number of Iraqi Civil Defense Forces trained, number of local government councils established, amount of civil affairs projects or money spent are all examples of the types of quantifiable data used to make assessments and recognize trends.

The most significant and emotionally charged metric was the number of U.S. casualties or deaths. Nothing was sure to attract the attention of a higher HQ like the number of U.S. deaths or casualties at the hands of the insurgents. There is nothing wrong with using this metric per se, but over time, and without an operational framework or campaign plan with a clearly defined endstate to work from, Coalition Forces became caught up playing the proverbial game of "whack a mole", i.e. throwing the irresistible force that is the U.S. Army sledgehammer against an enemy that often had already moved to another area. This occurred again and again in places like Tarmiyah, Sammara and Mosul, which as of 2009 was the place where the insurgency was most firmly entrenched despite being a backwater of the war from a U.S. military perspective for much of the preceding six years. Despite many indicators to the contrary, the lack of soldier deaths from insurgent attack in Tarmiyah in 2003 and early 2004 ensured the area would get little notice.

Even with a clear vision and using the proper metrics to measure success, and assuming a more experienced staff, nothing would have overcome the paucity of troops on the ground in 2003 and 2004. While more troops on the ground by themselves certainly wouldn't have ensured that victory, or at least conditions of peace, had prevailed, it at least would have brought victory into the realm of possibility. Without the leaders and soldiers to conduct the patrols, train the Iraqi security forces, secure the meetings, hunt the insurgents, protect the bases and most importantly interact with the population on a consistent basis, even the most comprehensive and nuanced counterinsurgency plan is doomed to failure.

While it was repeatedly touted by military and civilian leaders in the press that more combat troops were not needed nor requested by the Army senior leadership in 2003, the facts on the ground belied the rhetoric. In the case of Task Force Bear, responsible at one point for well over 1,200 square kilometers of terrain including MSR Tampa and several population centers, two additional companies totaling approximately two-hundred soldiers were needed to accomplish all its specified and implied tasks; the most important of which was securing and thereby influencing the Iraqi population. The fact is no one ever asked the Task Force Commanders and lower level staffs if they needed more soldiers. As of March 2004 there was no bottom up review done to discern or generate actual requirements. Internal to the Army there was little overt discussion or analysis on the need for more soldiers, and more of the right kind of soldiers. There was certainly no effort ever communicated to the mid-grade officers, who were acutely aware that a shortage of troops existed, that a formal process of review was underway or that anyone was championing this cause at higher levels.

How was this situation corrected? By the end of 2006 Coalition Forces finally had an operational framework to work from. Staffs and senior leaders had the experience and education to develop and apply the lessons learned from Vietnam, the Philippines, Algeria and Malaysia not to mention three years of fighting in Iraq. The ambiguous decisive operation of "Transition" (meaning literally transitioning bases and battle space to Iraqi forces, ready or not, in preparation for the impending U.S. withdrawal) was discarded for the strategy of securing Baghdad, which at least offered an opportunity for success. Through a series of operations and applying the theory *du jour* of "clear-hold-build" the U.S. Army began to implement its first comprehensive plan that offered a chance for winning. Recognizing at last that the population was decisive, and that the biggest portion of the Iraqi population, which also happened to be the seat of power, lived in Baghdad, securing Baghdad became the decisive operation. The now famous surge of 2007-2008, provided the troops that gave the strategy of securing Baghdad its first chance to succeed.

It took three years of fighting in Iraq to develop and communicate a vision that made sense to the lower level tactical units. Coupled with strategic benchmarks that defined an endstate and resourced with enough troops by way of the surge and the expansion of the Iraqi Security Forces' capabilities, Coalition Forces finally began to make significant progress.

That it took three years in Iraq and up to eight years in Afghanistan before the Army developed a plan with a chance of success magnifies the need for the Army to maintain a cadre of experts in different types of conflict. Just as there is now a central debate raging in the Army on how best to maintain the skills required to fight a high intensity, traditionally linear conflict after eight years of counterinsurgency fighting in Iraq and Afghanistan; there may at some time in the future be a debate about how to maintain the lessons learned from the wars in Iraq and Afghanistan as we become mired in a more traditional conflict.

One recommendation to address this dilemma is to segregate part of the force, perhaps several brigades, to focus solely on one type of contingency or the other. This force could expand and contract as needed based on the evolving threat. It would take the lead in any subsequent conflict where its specific skill set was predominant and provide cadres of trained officer and NCOs to quickly change or proliferate the needed skill-set to the remaining parts of the Army. For example, in 2010, if there was a sudden need to field a force proficient in high intensity warfare there are few brigades prepared to fight that type of engagement without a period of intense training. The amount of time needed to train and field such a force is pure speculation but there is no doubt the Army is currently ill prepared to fight a high intensity fight. Delineating at least a small part of the Army to focus on different contingencies at least begins to address the issue.

Leadership Lessons

- *Don't underestimate the need for a clearly communicated (i.e. understood) vision and endstate.*
- *There are some jobs that require more people to achieve success; at least as far as fighting an insurgency is concerned, technology has not replaced the need for significant numbers of people (i.e. soldiers) on the ground.*
- *Don't expect easy success from those without the training, education and experience for the assigned task.*
- *There are only two types of plans, those that might work and those that won't work-it always comes down to execution and execution requires the right people.*

Soldiers from Task Force Bear find a significant cache of 57mm rockets.

A typical cache of weapons. Rocket propelled grenade rounds shown.

TF Bear soldiers help Iraqi family during operations near Tarmiya in July 2003. (Chapter 3)

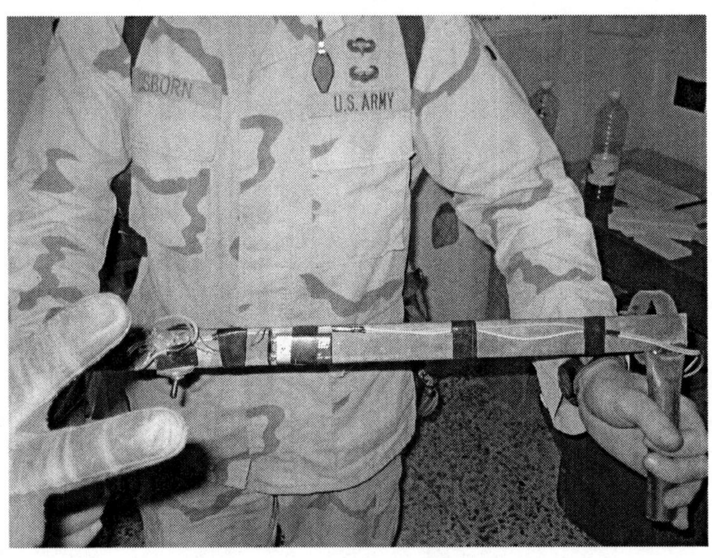

A captured example of an improvised 57mm rocket laucher without the rocket tubes. (Chapter 14)

Example of homemade detonators for IEDs. (Chapter 11)

The author (standing) listens to Bear Six (seated, far left) during planning for operations. (Chapter 2)

The author with member of the ICDC. Three of the ICDC members depicted were killed by insurgents within six months of photo. Another was suspected of cooperating with insurgents. (Chapter 13)

57mm rockets are recovered from a hidden cache. (Chapter 14)

Aerial of a typical Iraqi village.

A tank crushed 57mm rocket tubes used to make improvised rocket launchers. (Chapter 14)

Iraqi leaders meet to hold election.

The results of an IED attack. Fortunately, no one was seriously injured. (Chapter 11)

Iraqi leaders meet to hold election.

Task For Bear soldiers attempt to extract an M1A2 tank from an irrigation canal.

11

Counter-IED

THE PRIMARY REASON TASK FORCE BEAR WAS SENT TO the Tarmiyah area in the first place was to secure a section of Main Supply Route (MSR) Tampa from enemy attack. MRS Tampa was the main North to South route for U.S. Forces and Iraqis linking Baghdad to the cities of Mosul and Basra. It was also the main route linking large U.S. bases like FOB ANACONDA and TAJI, with populations sometimes reaching close to thirty thousand soldiers, Airmen and civilian contractors. North of Baghdad, MSR Tampa is a divided highway with two lanes of traffic running in each direction and a significant median. While sparsely traveled at its extremities, close in to Baghdad it is teaming with civilian cars and trucks of all kinds. In the mornings the road clogs with farmers' trucks and workers heading into the city. In the afternoons the flow is reversed. Early in the war, certainly throughout 2003, traffic on MSR Tampa after hours of darkness was limited, but this was largely dependent on the establishment and subsequent enforcement of any Coalition Forces imposed curfew.

IEDs or improvised explosive devices are, for lack of a simpler definition, bombs. In their most basic form they consist of an artillery or mortar round with an electrical blasting cap placed into the fuse-well, normally packed with an explosive like C4. The electrical blasting cap is tied through common electrical or speaker wire to a power source like a car battery. To detonate the IED, simply touch the ends of the wire to the car battery, initiating the blasting cap, which ignites the C4, which causes the artillery round to detonate. This type of IED is known as a command wired IED because it is manually detonated with a wire from the electrical source to the initiator. The triggerman is usually within a few hundred meters of the blast, but can be further away depending on the amount of electricity produced by his power source. In general, these types of IEDs are not particularly effective against armored vehicles though they certainly can't be ignored, particularly while dismounted.

All other IED types are variants to this basic model. IR triggers, victim initiated (think pressure plate IEDs and landmines), cell phone initiated, deep buried, vehicle borne IEDs, suicide IEDs, suicide vehicle IEDs (S-VBIEDs), sticky bombs, suicide vests, etc… are all types of IEDs encountered in Iraq. In 2003, the most common type of IED was composed of a 152 mm artillery round or a series of these rounds buried fuse-well (cone side) up, with wire leading to a power source. These were most often command detonated meaning the trigger man was on site, normally with direct observation of the IED engagement area. When the IEDs were placed in series, they occasionally included one or two rounds rigged with timers set to detonate sometime after the initial explosion. These were intended to target first responders, causing maximum casualties after soldiers and emergency personnel had dismounted from their vehicles to help the original victims.

Some of the most devastating IEDs early in the war were the "deep buried" IEDs. These IEDs often consisted of ten to twenty 152mm artillery rounds or hundreds of pounds of TNT equivalent that were buried beneath a dirt road. When these IEDs detonated the sheer size of the blast, as opposed to the shrapnel from the rounds, was usually fatal to the entire crew of even the heaviest armored vehicles. Fortunately, deep buried IEDs were not too common. They took a long time to emplace, and were resource intensive, usually depending on Coalition Forces to have set some kind of discernible pattern of movement in order to be effective.

Later, largely with the help of Iranian technology, a new type of IED, the EFP or explosively formed projectile became prevalent. The EFP was a machined weapon that could be aimed, thus making it much more effective. The slug from an EFP, traveling at a high rate of speed, acts like a miniature armor-piercing round that is an efficient killer when aimed correctly. Though most feared because of its high casualty rate, the EFP was akin to all other IEDs in terms of how it was employed, and therefore how it could be countered.

The only hundred-percent guaranteed way to avoid being hit with an IED was to stay on base. Even then though, eventually, the enemy would find some other way to attack you. Units that chose to take a more passive approach and/or consolidated on large bases became attacked with S-VBIEDs at the entry control points, with mortars or rockets or sniper attacks on the towers. More importantly, no war is ever won by staying on base and there was still a mission to accomplish. So if remaining on base in the hope of avoiding casualties and consequently abrogating the responsibility for prosecuting the war is not an option, the only other choice is to move out among the population. This automatically puts you at risk to an IED attack.

In any scenario you can remain passive, hoping things will work out in your favor; or you can take an aggressive role, get on the ground and influence the situation to your benefit. It is no different when attempting to counter Improvised Explosive Devices. Assuming that you really do want to prosecute the war successfully there is no avoiding the risks. That isn't to say that there aren't passive measures available. The Army did a commendable job outfitting units with jamming equipment, increasing armor protection, and outfitting HMMWVs with "rhinos" designed to trip an IR IED early so the blast doesn't impact the crew compartment of the vehicle. These are all useful devices and all work, but none are a panacea. The technology available to insurgents has continued to adapt to each new passive measure employed. The only way to win then is to actively mitigate the attack through offensive action. The three basic options are to own the terrain, clear the terrain, or bypass the terrain.

The easiest way to illustrate these concepts is to think of the blast area or kill zone of an IED as an enemy engagement area. An engagement area in U.S. Army doctrinal terms is a place on the ground where the effects of weapons systems are massed to defeat an enemy. Engagement areas are normally chosen because they naturally channelize the enemy along limited avenues of approach and provide good observation and fields of fire to the defender. Well-developed engagement areas are normally marked with reference points that are used as triggers so defenders know exactly when to shoot and when their weapons will have the most effect. Often there are man-made or natural obstacles that protect the defenders and allow them to engage and if necessary withdraw without being destroyed by the attacker. The last set of factors in the defender's favor is that he gets to choose the time, place and object of the attack. Compounding these natural advantages to the adept defender is today's IED technology, which allows a triggerman to initiate an IED without being present at the site of the attack. With such advantages, it should be abundantly clear why IEDs pose such a persistent and deadly problem that even the best military minds and technological improvements have been unable to overcome.

Owning the terrain is the simplest concept to master but the most resource intensive to put into practice. Owning the terrain implies constant presence, either through active patrolling, traffic control points picketed along likely IED engagement areas, manned observation posts overwatching those same IED engagement areas or some sort of technological observation provided by unmanned aircraft or long range cameras. In later years a combination of the techniques listed above were used effectively. With the proliferation of technology and the increase in capabilities of the Iraqi Security Forces the need for Coalition patrols was significantly reduced.

For Task Force Bear in 2003, however, patrolling was the main deterrent with almost constant presence on MSR Tampa required to curb the number and effectiveness of IED attacks. Many times overlapping patrols were used; that is two patrols operating in close proximity, often on parallel routes, or one patrol operating with an element forward, the "hunter", and another element to the rear, known as the "killer". The intent of these patrols was to goad the enemy to fixate on the lead element so the trail or parallel element could find, fix and destroy them. It was taken for granted that the element moving through the likely engagement area, the "hunters", were at great risk of getting attacked. Variants of this technique included use of air weapons teams (AWT) or UAV in overwatch, shutting down vehicles and/or moving very slowly in blackout drive to reduce the noise and light signature of the patrol and sometimes using dismounted elements moving on parallel routes. All of these techniques were regularly conducted with the intent of catching someone in the act of emplacing the IED.

Initially the technique of owning the terrain worked fairly well. Insurgents unaware of U.S. technological advantages or tactics were sometimes caught or killed as they worked to emplace an IED on the side of the road. After several months, however, as the untrained or careless insurgents were killed off, the enemy adapted more creative emplacement techniques.

The most effective adaptation was to build the IED in stages with one individual responsible for laying in the explosives in a cache, another responsible for making and delivering the initiation device, and a third responsible for digging the hole and/or sighting in and prepping the engagement area with triggers and obstacles. With the IED fully assembled and the engagement area prepped, it took a relatively short period of time for the final emplacement, certainly less than a couple of minutes. With alert observers signaling the approach of U.S. forces, the insurgents would blend into the population and wait for a U.S. patrol to pass before conducting the final emplacement. The theory being that those minutes directly after a U.S. patrol had passed provided the best chance to emplace an IED undetected. As building the IED engagement area was stretched over several days, changes in the roadways were not readily noticed by soldiers on patrol. They got used to seeing the same hole or pile of debris on the side of the road. After initially checking the area for IEDs over several patrols, units eventually disregarded the area as a threat. There are numerous examples of the same IED hole being used repeatedly and with success against U.S. patrols.

Another option open to the insurgents was to simply move outside the actively patrolled areas. These seams between units, tied to military boundaries and often used as turnaround points for patrols, became well known to the enemy. By operating just outside the patrolled areas the insurgents could act with near impunity. On MSR Tampa the high amount of Coalition Forces traffic meant the insurgents could avoid local U.S. "combat" forces like Task Force Bear, allowing them to pass, in order to target one of the larger logistics patrols moving up and down the route throughout the day. These patrols were at a disadvantage because of their size, lack of combat platforms and most importantly their lack of situational awareness about the area. They were also an attractive target because they did not have the mission or the combat power needed to pursue the enemy once attacked. The insurgents could be confident that if they attacked a large logistics patrol there wouldn't be any sustained return fire nor would anyone pursue them. All the insurgents would have to do was to lay low, wait for the inevitable burst of gunfire from the over anxious machine gunners and then blend into the population. In fact the large logistics patrols rarely stopped unless forced to because of damage to a vehicle or casualties.

As enemy techniques developed the insurgents became skilled at removing asphalt in the middle of a road by pouring gasoline into a puddle and setting it on fire. In a matter of minutes the asphalt would melt enough to allow it to be dug up. The IED would be emplaced and covered over with fresh asphalt. The entire process could be completed in a matter of minutes. Another favorite technique was to emplace IEDs in the carcasses of dead animals.

Despite these enemy adaptations Task Force Bear accomplished its essential task of securing their section of MSR Tampa. While IED attacks continued, with as many as five a day on the relatively short 25km stretch of highway, no deaths from IEDs in Task Force Bear's section of MSR Tampa occurred in nine months of combat operations there. While not able to completely eradicate IED attacks, the frequency of patrols forced the enemy to rely on hastily emplaced, and therefore less effective, IEDs.

The toll of constant patrolling on U.S. soldiers and equipment was heavy both in terms of psychological stresses and damage to vehicles. The mission was made even more difficult in late 2003 and early 2004 when the Army decided to consolidate forces away from smaller outposts onto large bases. The intent here was twofold: first to reduce logistics costs and improve security by removing the need to support remote bases; and second to reduce the amount of close contact U.S. soldiers had with the Iraqi population in the hope of reducing tensions. For Task Force Bear this meant closing Patrol Base Animal located mere meters from MSR Tampa at the intersection of Highway One and the main route into Tarmiyah. Without this key base, it became more difficult to secure the route, QRF response times were quadrupled and control of the area in general was reduced.

The overall effect of removing U.S forces from close proximity to the population helped contribute to the rise in sectarian problems later in the war; the near term impact was how it negatively affected the counter IED fight. Fortunately for U.S. forces, a new TTP was emerging, the route clearance team.

Route Clearance Teams were developed specifically to counter the burgeoning IED threat in late 2003. At the most basic, ad hoc level, these were nothing more than standard patrols sent forward of logistic or other movements to clear or "proof" a route. For Task Force Bear this meant that tanks or sometimes infantry fighting vehicles, the most heavily armored vehicles available, would lead patrols to clear routes, especially into Tarmiyah, ahead of scheduled patrols to meetings or civil affairs visits. For the main routes like MSR Tampa, engineer units were reconfigured and given route clearance as a primary task. Early in the war, without the specialized route clearance equipment later purchased and distributed throughout the force, the most prevalent technique used by the engineers was the dismounted patrol. Walking just off the routes, normally at night, these patrols attempted to identify the command wires, new holes, caches and enemy overwatch sites before the IEDs could be fully prepared and emplaced.

Not infrequently, soldiers working dismounted around suspected or historic IED engagement areas often stumbled onto IEDs; literally standing on top of the IED before recognizing what it was and backing off. The IEDs were often so well concealed that they were difficult to detect. In one such case, during a reconnaissance of a historic IED engagement area along route COBRA outside of Tarmiyah the Apache Company commander, Apache 6, was dismounted, showing a fellow commander where and how the enemy emplaced IEDs. While pointing out a specific hole that had been previously used to hide IEDs, Apache 6 was surprised to find that the hole had already been reseeded. They were standing just a few feet away from an IED. Fortunately it wasn't yet complete for detonation.

Enemy tactics also evolved to meet the increased scrutiny of the RCT. A favorite TTP was to stage a broken down vehicle on the side of the road, using the cover of ongoing vehicle repairs to set the ambush. Another was to place IEDs along guardrails and other elevated points in an attempt to increase casualties and counter our fixation on holes in the ground. Insurgents also used dummy or hoax IEDs to get patrols to stop and react, while the real IED was positioned to attack those focused on the hoax. IEDs on delayed timers and enhanced with double switched initiating devices that caused the bomb to detonate if tampered with were also used. On one patrol, Task Force Bear soldiers were targeted by a vehicle borne IED that was staged on the side of the road as a broken down vehicle. Only a last second maneuver by the lead HMMWV driver prevented more significant casualties.

U.S. and Task Force Bear tactics also evolved. Engineers used their earth moving assets along route Tampa to reduce vegetation and uneven terrain that could hide IEDs. Suspected enemy overwatch sites became targeted areas of interest (TAIs) with dedicated assets to observe them during suspected emplacement or attack times. Trash cleanup projects had the dual purpose of making Iraqi towns more sanitary and livable, but also removed potential camouflage used to hide the bombs. Previously used holes were marked with spray paint as a warning to patrols traveling through the area that they were entering an IED engagement area. As the IED fight matured U.S. combat units travelled with "quickcrete" concrete, which was used to immediately fill potential or historic IED holes during routine patrols. Eventually the proliferation of small robots and large anti-mine, anti-IED vehicles like the "Buffalo", outfitted with an interrogating arm and camera, dramatically improved the survivability of U.S. soldiers conducting the counter-IED fight, and freed combat units from the constant patrolling necessary for terrain denial.

Of course the enemy adapted its TTP again, finally employing EFPs on infrared (IR) triggers that could be emplaced in a matter of minutes and turned on and off (armed) by remote control. Without a technological or organizational answer to the EFP, units migrated to the third option available in the counter-IED fight, avoidance.

Bypassing the enemy IED engagement area seems the most obvious and easiest way to defeat IED effects. Unfortunately, it is a much more difficult concept to put into practice. The fact is that many of the same IED engagement areas that were used in 2003 and 2004 in and around Tarmiyah were still causing casualties through 2008. There are a number of contributing factors. With regard to IED engagement areas along MSR Tampa, there simply aren't any feasible bypasses for much of the route. While bypasses do exist on route Cobra into Tarmiyah, they are significantly slower and much more congested. Units that hadn't spent much time in Tarmiyah, or hadn't done adjacent unit coordination wouldn't necessarily know of these bypass routes because they aren't readily apparent on a map. Many of the routes also don't support large vehicle movement for vehicles like fuel trucks, tanks, or even MRAPs. Additionally, as soon as these alternate routes became frequently used they too would become targeted. Sometimes moving down a particular route is simply unavoidable. There are meetings with local Iraqis and city governments to conduct. Most U.S. bases are only accessible from certain routes. Sometimes you travel through an IED ambush engagement area because you are *trying* to gain contact with the enemy and/or are rapidly moving to the aid of a friendly unit under attack.

The most effective way to avoid being hit with an IED then is to avoid setting patterns by varying routes and times of movement. Varying road-march speeds make it difficult for the enemy to coordinate the timing of an attack or to properly aim the weapon. Making unpredictable tactical stops or u-turns confuses the enemy as to the intent of the mission. Changing the location and times of regular meetings will cause the enemy to seek more predictable targets. Showing up early, or if the situation allows, arriving late will try the enemy's patience and disrupt his attack timing. At a minimum, units should never move through an area without first doing coordination on attack patterns with the local unit. Most enemy IED cells have their own battle rhythm and planning cycle. Attacks will most often occur between certain times or on certain days for any given engagement area. Figure out what these are and plan movement around them.

Even after all of these methods are exhausted, there will still be missions requiring units to move through active IED engagement areas. In these cases the movement needs to be planned and deliberate. Units must change movement formations and techniques prior to entering the engagement area, just like they would in a high intensity fight. Dismounts should be employed. Overwatch established by supporting ground teams, AWT or UAV. Route clearance teams should be pushed out front to clear the ground. It is a deliberate, resource intensive operation.

Another option in the counter-IED fight: is to immerse and surround the patrol within and among the civilian population. This was a technique practiced with varying degrees of success by different units throughout Iraq from early 2003 and was almost exclusively adopted by 2009. While some areas and units favored big convoys with large standoff distances from local vehicles, others allowed civilian vehicles to intertwine themselves with U.S. movements. One favorite technique during the later years of the war was for U.S. patrols to get behind a large Iraqi truck or other vehicle and simply follow it. In this way, insurgents had to decide if they wanted to risk killing civilians when they tried to target a U.S. patrol.

Curfews were another tactic impacting the IED fight and were used with different application and success in different parts of Iraq. From the IED fight perspective curfews certainly played into the hands of the enemy. Since all civilian traffic had to be off the roads by 2000 hours the enemy was assured that any vehicle movement beyond that time would be Coalition Forces. Sole use of roads by military units at night led to the proliferation of the very deadly pressure plate IEDs in 2005 and 2006; and later, to the preference of the enemy to use IR initiators. The effectiveness of these types of IEDs was greatly curtailed once civilian traffic was able to travel the roads at all times of the day and night. The enemy was then faced with the potential for causing civilian casualties when targeting U.S. forces. While AQI may not have been deterred by the specter of civilian casualties, most Shia based groups avoided them, and the Shia groups were the ones who most employed EFPs. Most insurgents had done their homework. They knew they couldn't win their fight if the population was alienated. There were certainly times when a curfew was necessary to help control the security situation, but the universal application of curfews made attacking U.S. forces with IEDs, especially at night, far easier.

Detractors would point out that that the technique of allowing civilian traffic to move in and around a Coalition Forces convoy opens it up to attack from a S-VBIED. However, the fact remains that far more soldiers were killed from IEDs than S-VBIEDs directed against U.S. patrols. Additionally, an S-VBIED doesn't need to integrate into a U.S. patrol to be effective; it could simply wait for the U.S. patrol to pass by before the driver guns the engine and detonates himself against one of the patrol's vehicles. Again, having civilian traffic interspersed and moving around the friendly patrol may inhibit or dissuade the potential attacker.

None of these tactics, techniques or procedures is a

panacea. In fact many would argue that the real way to defeat an IED is to attack the cell that is paying for the supplies, transporting them into the county and putting them together; that once the IED is in place it is already too late. There is certainly a lot of merit to this argument and much effort goes into attacking insurgent cells. Despite these efforts and untold millions of U.S. dollars being put against the IED fight, as of this writing IEDs still account for the largest proportion of C.F. deaths. This is a repeating trend in Afghanistan.

Perhaps the most important factors that eventually led to the precipitous drop in IED attacks later in the war were the growing capabilities of the indigenous security forces, the Iraqi Army and Police, who by then had picketed nearly all historic IED engagement areas, and the increased U.S. effort to secure the borders, particularly with Iran, thereby disrupting the flow of lethal aid. The influence of the mostly Sunni Awakening Councils, or "Sahwa", also needs to be recognized as a significant contributor to the drop in IED attacks. In many cases the Sahwa initiative was nothing more than the U.S. Army paying former insurgents not to conduct IED attacks. The program was unquestionably and significantly successful. Official recognition of the Sunni resistance as a legitimate part of the Iraqi security equation was later co-opted by the Iraqi government as the lynchpin to the Sunni-Shia reconciliation that is still ongoing.

In purely military context, IEDs are merely another weapon system. As deadly and horrific as they are, they never succeeded in causing more than a handful of U.S. casualties at any given time. As a weapon then, they were not decisive enough to defeat U.S. Army tactical units. However, the psychological cost of soldiers constantly on patrol, susceptible to attack without warning and without the immediate satisfaction of being able to fight back directly contributed to the high levels of frustration and stress felt by the many soldiers who spent up to 12 hours a day conducting counter-IED patrols. This psychological cost coupled with the amount of resources tied up fighting the IED problem provided a substantial operational, and quite nearly strategic success for the enemy at relatively low cost. This is the continuing legacy of the counter-IED fight, a legacy that is impacting the way the U.S. Army prepares for future wars.

Leadership Lessons

- *Be unpredictable to the enemy, even when what you are doing is working.*
- *Keep adapting or your enemy will gain the initiative; the one with the initiative wins.*
- *Risk can never be completely eliminated (only mitigated); if the level of risk is not acceptable and is therefore preventing the accomplishment of the mission then the worth of the mission needs to be reevaluated.*
- *Don't rely on technological improvements; the IED fight is a clear example of a technological arms race, with each side developing new technologies to counter the other's advancements; while technological advancements were significant and must be pursued, the most effective adaptations were not technologically based.*

12

Doing the Right Thing

IN 2003 FOB ANACONDA WAS A BLACK HOLE FOR COMBAT power. As one of the largest logistics hubs with one of the most capable airstrips in Iraq, preventing rocket and mortar fire against the base was a high priority. To counter these attacks it was directed to place a series of observation posts (OPs) around the FOB to cover historic points of origin (POOs). The problem with this type of fixed observation plan was that the enemy soon realized where the OPs were and simply shifted to other attack locations. This in turn led to higher HQs directing a new OP to cover the latest POO, a pattern that repeated itself and soon strained the available combat power of Task Force Bear and other units surrounding the base.

In addition to taxing available combat power, the stationary OPs provided easy targets for the enemy as they observed U.S. troops moving to the same areas along the same routes on a daily basis. Task Force Bear and other battalion task forces resisted stationary OPs in favor of more active, less predictive patrolling and took measures to vary routes and locations as much as possible. To help the Task Force with its paucity of combat power, the Brigade would send other troops to assist with the OP missions whenever possible. The fate of one such element, the LRRS, was detailed in a previous chapter. In this case the Brigade deployed a Ground Surveillance Radar (GSR) team to establish an observation post overwatching a recent mortar firing point. The GSR team was not attached to TF Bear and received no guidance from it. It was required to operate on the TF Bear radio frequency in case they needed support from a QRF or medical evacuation but otherwise acted independently.

On a linear battlefield the GSR team normally operates as part of a screen line, incorporated into the overall security operation as just one of a number of complimentary sensors. In this case the team was being asked to operate independently and provide its own security, not relying on their electronic sensors but acting in the more traditional ground OP role normally preformed by Army Scouts. The result was that they occupied precisely the same location, at the same time, using the exact same routes each time they conducted the mission. The team also failed to clear the surrounding area or push out any dismounted security. While Task Force Bear soldiers had conducted similar operations for almost two months without enemy contact, the actions of the GSR team were so predictable that after only five days they were ambushed. At approximately 2130 hours:

"Sir, we're getting reports of contact from the GSR team."

"What do we got?"

"Mortars and small arms fire."

"That doesn't sound right... Mortars... probably RPGs or grenades..."

"Bear X-ray, this is QRF. We're REDCON one."

"This is Bear 3. Roger. Are you tracking the contact?"

"Affirmative. We monitored all."

"Roger, move now, break..."

"Stalker, this is Bear 3."

"This is Stalker. Over"

"I need three trucks at REDCON 1."

"Roger..."

From Bear 3 to the TOC NCOIC: *"Let's call BDE and*

let them know, see if any aircraft are available... and get my truck ready."

"Bear 3, this is Bandit X-ray"

"Bandit X-ray, Bear 3"

"Bandit 6 is standing up a truck and wants to move with you." There were Bandit 6's soldiers on the QRF and he wanted in on the action.

"This is Bear 3. Roger"

"Bear X-ray, this is OP 1 request a MEDEVAC. 9 line to follow."

"Damn, this is Bear 3. Standby on the 9 line. What is the injury?"

"We've got one soldier with a gunshot wound to the hand."

"Roger. QRF is inbound less than five minutes out... Recommend ground evac straight to Anaconda. It'll be quicker... Can we get a SITREP?"

"Roger. A couple of explosions followed by small arms fire from the east, we returned fire, our team leader is hit."

"This is Bear 3. Is it life threatening?"

"This is OP 1. Negative."

"Any BDA?"

"Negative at this time."

"This is Bear 3. Roger. Speak to QRF this net and guide them in."

"Roger."

A minute later…

"Any Bear? This is Gunslinger 1-1 (AWT)."

"Gunslinger, this is Bear 3. Go ahead."

"Bear 3, this is Gunslinger 1-1. We've got two AH64s inbound. Can we get a SITREP?"

"This is Bear 3. We've got troops in contact vicinity mike-charlie-three-three-two-eight-six-niner. I say again: three-three-two-eight-six-niner. We've got small arms and possible RPGs, break. Speak to Bear QRF on this frequency. They are inbound."

"This is Gunslinger 1-1. Roger."

Several minutes later…

"*Bear X-ray, this is QRF. We have linked up with the OP. CONTACT! CONTACT. East out!"*

Several minutes later, with the secondary QRF at REDCON 1:

"Bear *X-ray, this is Bear 3. Five vehicles, 17 personnel SP FOB. Bear in route to the OP"*

"This is Bear X-ray. Roger"

"QRF, this is Bear 3, SITREP. Over"

Silence.

"*QRF, this is Bear 3, SITREP. Over"*

Silence.

"*Bear 3, this is Gunslinger 1-1. We've got eyes on the contact. It looks like at least one bad guy. Request permission to fire."*

"Roger. We need to get the QRF on the net. They are in charge on the ground and need to clear fires."

"Bear 3, this is QRF. We've got small arms contact... White 4 is on the ground."

"Roger. Speak to Gunslinger. They are prepared to support."

A short while later:

"*Bear 3, this is Gunslinger 1-1. Rounds on the way."*

Rockets and .50 Cal fire raining down from the sky, in the darkness seemingly out of nowhere.

"*Bear 3, this is Gunslinger 1-1."*

"Bear 3."

"*This is Gunslinger 1-1. We're BINGO on ammunition... We're observing one individual laying down about 100m east of the QRF position. Not sure if he's alive."*

"This is Bear 3. Roger."

"This is Gunslinger 1-1. We've got about 10 minutes left on fuel and need to return to base. We'll be back up in about thirty minutes"

"This is Bear 3. Roger. Thanks for the help."

"Bear 3, this is QRF. We're moving through the

objective. Negative contact at this time."

"This is Bear 3. Roger. Did you get the report of possible enemy lying to your east about 100 meters?"

"This is QRF. Roger."

"This is Bear 3. We'll be on the ground in a minute..."

Bear 3 jumped from his truck as the aircraft were breaking station.

"Where is White 4?"

"Over there, sir," pointing.

Coming up on White Four: *"Sergeant C, what've we got?"*

"One wounded bad guy, sir, over here."

"You okay?"

*"F***er shot at me."*

"Did you get him?"

"Yeah, he's not dead, but pretty tore up."

The insurgent lay on the ground, bandoleer of ammunition across his chest, RPG launcher with extra rounds laying next to him with an AK47. A chunk of the side of his skull was missing. Several other bullet holes and injuries; intestines spilled out. He was struggling to breathe, eyes glassy and far away.

At least four U.S. soldiers on their hands and knees around the wounded enemy, medical kit spread out, trying to save his life. American soldiers and medics are trained in combat life saving skills. They are also trained that once an enemy is incapacitated and is no longer a threat; they will be given medical care.

Bear 3 looked around. *"What the f**k are we doing here?"*

The soldiers looked up, undoubtedly thinking it was obvious what they were doing.

"Who is pulling security... Sergeant, have we cleared through this area yet?"

"No, sir, we came up on this guy and started working on him"

"OKAY, stop... Stop working on him. I want this area

secured... We need to clear out to that canal. What about those buildings over there? Look, there's probably more bad guys out here. Get some of Stalker and get this area secure."

"WILCO, sir."

"Where is the medic? He can keep working on this guy; everyone else pulls security and clears the area." Bear 3 looks at the wounded Iraqi. "*I don't think he's going to make it anyway."*

The insurgent was mortally wounded and didn't survive more than a few minutes. After clearing the area without further incident, they loaded the dead body on a stretcher and strapped him to the hood of Bear 3's HMMWV for transport back to the FOB. Better that than generate another patrol to bring out an ambulance. As Task Force Bear departed the area a fire was set to a pile of hay near where the insurgent was killed; an admittedly weak attempt to send a message to the locals about not supporting insurgents. This type of retribution while questionably effective was surprisingly therapeutic.

The GSR team never returned to conduct future OP missions. The reality was they weren't particularly well trained for that type of operation and didn't have the leadership needed within their organization to make sure they were properly prepared. The immediate response of the QRF and the availability and responsiveness of the helicopters sent a clear message to any nearby enemy. It was the last direct fire attack against an OP in the Task Force Bear area of operations for the duration of their deployment.

Leadership Lessons

- *Subordinates may be doing the right thing (e.g. trying to save the life of a wounded enemy combatant), but that may still not be what you need them to be doing.*

- *It is the leaders job to understand the bigger picture and direct his subordinates accordingly.*
- *Don't assume outside organizations share standard operating procedures or core competencies. If they are going to be working in your area, make sure you find out.*

13

ICDC

IN THE SPRING OF 2003, A DECISION WAS MADE TO DISband the Iraqi Army and other ministry of defense forces. The merits of this decision have been chronicled and debated in numerous books, on television news shows and in political forums. For battalions, companies and platoons fighting in Iraq, the implications of this decision were far reaching.

For instance, a considerable number of U.S. soldiers and equipment were initially involved in safeguarding the huge stores of Iraqi munitions left over from the war. These munitions were not only scattered in remote sites, but were also stored in and around existing military bases. Task Force Bear lived in and created a base around the old ammunition bunkers of an Iraqi Air Force ammunition depot (on Iraqi maps referred to as the Balad Ammunition Storage Point (ASP)). Since the thousands of rockets, cluster bombs and missiles posed a serious risk to U.S. soldiers, not to mention a potential threat if pilfered by the enemy, there was a considerable effort made not only to safeguard the weapons but also to dispose of them. All of this required countless man-hours of time that could otherwise have been devoted to interacting with and securing the population. In fact the mere presence and quantity of ammunition at places like FOB Bear drove units to occupy and stay in those areas when there was no other tactical reason to do so.

While there may be some doubt as to whether or how much the Iraqi Army could have been trusted to guard sites like these on their own, particularly before the capture of Saddam, the fact that there wasn't a pool of Iraqi soldiers and military leaders to draw from led to a significant degradations in U.S. capability. Coupled with the ineptness of the Iraqi Police Forces (who should be thought of more as an armed fire department, venturing outside their stations only after being called or when ordered to do so by a judge) the lack of Iraqi Army troops drew U.S. forces into guarding Iraqi infrastructure such as pipelines, electrical plants even gas stations. This is clearly not a mission U.S. commanders wanted their soldiers conducting. U.S. soldiers were neither trained for nor particularly fond of this type of static security task.

By August of 2003 Coalition Forces had come up with a plan to alleviate the burden of providing force protection and local infrastructure security. The plan attempted to co-opt the local male population by hiring and training them to perform basic security tasks. A secondary effect of the effort was as a jobs program that put money into the hands of the community and, hopefully, engendered them to the U.S. presence. For those familiar with the Awakening Councils, "Sawha" in Arabic, or the Sons of Iraq program that began in Anbar province in 2005, this was a similar if not identical effort that enticed different segments of the population to participate. In 2003, it was mainly Shia groups that were eager to assert themselves in the wake of the pro-Sunni Ba'athist regime of Saddam Hussein.

In the Tarmiyah and Mushaedah areas, where Task Force Bear operated, initial response was promising. There was no shortage of volunteers for the first round of training in August 2003. Candidates had to pass a nominal physical exam and had to be able to read and write. Their names were also run through the U.S. intelligence system for possible links to the old regime or known terrorist cells.

Former Baathists were not allowed to apply.

The non-commissioned officers of Task Force Bear took the lead in training the Iraqis, running a modified basic training course that included military customs and courtesies, drill and ceremony, basic rifle marksmanship, basic human rights training and several security related tasks. Given the significant challenge of instructing students who spoke a different language and the need to overcome cultural realities (for example: if a recruit was yelled at or humiliated in front of his peers for making repeated mistakes, a standard practice in traditional U.S. Army basic training, the Iraqi student may very well not return to training because he had been publicly shamed) the training proceeded well and the recruits were generally responsive.

There were problems however. On at least two occasions suspected insurgents who were wanted in connection with attacks on U.S. forces tried to join the training program. These men were allowed to join and then subsequently arrested when they arrived at the training. Other recruits were turned in by their classmates for boasting about their plans to use the training and uniform to attack Coalition Forces. These problems were potentially serious but were not wide spread enough to derail the training process. It was encouraging that the recruits felt comfortable enough with their American trainers to turn in members of their own community.

As the months progressed, additional groups of recruits were trained until there were eventually close to two hundred trained ICDC on the roles. The ICDC officers were chosen from the most promising recruits. Some even had prior military experience. As it turned out, training the Iraqis, while challenging, proved easier than getting the ICDC soldiers to conduct themselves as a professional unit once they had graduated.

The first ICDC commander, Waleed, was chosen from among the initial class of recruits largely because of his prior military experience as an Iraqi non-commissioned officer. He was able to perform drill and ceremony, knew military structure and administrative procedures and at least while in class was able to get the other recruits to do what he said. With few options, and a reluctance by others to step forward, Waleed became the commander almost by default. He lasted less than six weeks.

Problems were immediately apparent. Once outside of the training environment, and watchful, constant American presence, the other ICDC soldiers followed Waleed reluctantly. It seems that although Task Force Bear had bestowed the rank of commanding officer on him, he commanded little respect and held little influence with the local community or with the informal tribal hierarchy. Waleed's power rested solely in his relationship with the American forces. When outside the U.S. sphere of influence, the average ICDC soldier knew that Waleed held no power. He couldn't reprimand or order an ICDC member to do something the soldier didn't want to do because of the societal and tribal backlash Waleed would face.

Compounding Waleed's societal impotence were his own actions. Barely had the first pay period passed when the Task Force Bear leadership began getting reports that Waleed was extorting money. Not only was he taking money from the existing ICDC soldiers, but he was taxing aspiring recruits. Telling them that if they didn't pay him his pittance he would make sure they weren't hired.

That this type of graft was prevalent in Iraqi society and was not a surprise to Task Force Bear. What was a surprise, however, was that Waleed would so quickly and unabashedly resort to demanding money when he had been warned explicitly against doing so before being appointed ICDC commander. In another strike against Waleed, the local chief of police had received complaints that ICDC soldiers sent to guard and help control access to the local gas station were extorting money from customers. The

ICDC soldiers would bump people to the front of the queue in exchange for a few Iraqi Dinar at a time when distribution of gasoline was a problem throughout Iraq. Again the money trail led back to the commander, "Captain" Waleed.

The subsequent firing of Waleed turned out to be a benefit for Task Force Bear as the new ICDC commander carried more influence with the local community. Waleed was asked to report to Bear 3. He was given the choice of staying with the ICDC as a non-commissioned officer or resigning from the force altogether. Completely shamed and unable to face his former subordinates at a reduced rank he chose the latter. He left the base with tears in his eyes after pleading for a second chance. He was never seen by TF Bear again.

After Waleed was fired and the attack on the Tarmiyah police station, the ICDC faced its first series of serious challenges. The local insurgents felt threatened by this new Iraqi security force that had been trained by Americans. Slowly, as the effectiveness of the ICDC improved and became more of a force for security in the Tarmiyah Qadah, the insurgents faced an indigenous challenge to their influence over the local population. The new crop of leaders for the ICDC included several more prominent men from the small Shia community around Tarmiyah. As previously discussed, Tarmiyah is a mostly Sunni enclave, but as in most of Iraq there are members of other sects living among the community. In 2003 the rift and tension between the two religious communities was not appreciated as the potential flash point that it was.

The Sunni insurgents around Tarmiyah, feeling threatened by this new force that fell outside their influence, began striking back. The first step they took was to kidnap one of the ICDC leaders, Abdulla, who disappeared in November 2003. Incensed that one of their own had been kidnapped, the ICDC seized the initiative for the first time and began conducting searches in the local community in the hopes of finding and freeing Abdulla. This was done without overt U.S. involvement and was hailed at the time as a step forward.

While conducting the searches, the ICDC stumbled onto several Iraqis in the process of moving a large shipment of weapons and ammunition from one hide position to another. When confronted, the men moving the weapons cache fired on the ICDC with their AK 47s, killing one before fleeing. This was a significant emotional event in Tarmiyah because it marked the first open killing of Iraqi by Iraqi.

Through follow up investigations Task Force Bear learned that the weapons smugglers were well known in the area. At the time it was believed by the locals that the weapons smugglers would leave their neighbors alone as long as business interests weren't disrupted. The murder of the ICDC soldier, who was well known and well liked in the local community, resulted in a public call for reconciliation and an end to Iraqi on Iraqi violence in the area. An agreement on an end to Iraqi on American violence proved more allusive.

Despite the agreement, attacks on ICDC increased with several more deaths and kidnappings in the subsequent months. By January 2004 attacks against ICDC and Iraqi police eclipsed attacks against Task Force Bear and other Coalition soldiers in the surrounding area. At about the same time the remains of Abdulla, hair and teeth, were believed recovered from a house on the outskirts of the Qada. Ominous signs of things to come in Tarmiyah.

Shortly after the uptick in violence against the ICDC, the new commander, Abbas, reported that he had worked out a deal with the local leaders so that the ICDC would no longer be attacked. Unfortunately this agreement coincided with a drop off in ICDC effectiveness and willingness to support Coalition Forces operations. Their standards at traffic control points diminished, arrests and leads dropped off. It came to be suspected that in his agreement with the local leaders, Abbas had also given up his willingness to actively oppose the insurgents.

Around the same time word came down from higher headquarters that the ICDC should be pushed to become more of an independent unit, taking on unilateral operations. This decision was made despite the lack of any existing Iraqi structure to provide pay and logistics or effectively assert command and control over the force. While the ICDC were being asked to assume a more substantial and independent role in area security, Task Force Bear was being told to close down Patrol Base Animal and consolidate its forces. These two opposing initiatives led to the development of a plan to hand over the patrol base to the ICDC command in February 2004, making it one of the first autonomous Iraqi bases in the country. (Note: On 14 October 2004, a mortar attack killed four and wounded up to eighty Iraqi National Guard soldiers at the patrol base in Mushahida; the outpost was subsequently shut down)

Following the turnover of Patrol Base Animal to the ICDC in early February 2004 Task Force Bear maintained daily contact and supervision of the ICDC. This was necessary not only because the fledgling Iraqi force relied on Task Force Bear for all its support, including pay, ammunition, weapons, uniforms, sand bags, vehicles and training, but because it also had serious deficiencies in discipline and standards. A visit by Bear 3 to the ICDC compound in the days following the handover, highlighted these deficiencies.

Driving through the Iraqi entry control point on his way into the compound Bear 3 was pleased to see Iraqis manning their weapons and alert at the front gate. They had parked one of their vehicles across the entry control point to prevent any S-VBIED from crashing through and had a PKC machine gun displayed on the roof of the truck. The first three Iraqis he saw were even in their uniform shirts, though they were not wearing their bulletproof vests or helmets. On closer inspection however it was clear something wasn't right. There was no ammunition loaded in the PKC. In fact, none of the three ICDC soldiers at the front gate had any ammunition. When confronted they said they had each shot their weapons the night before at insurgents trying to attack the base. A report that immediately aroused suspicion. Why hadn't the ammunition been replaced? The soldiers lamented that their leaders refused to issue any more ammunition and were requiring them to purchase their own from the local market, something they complained they couldn't afford to do because of their low pay and the high price of ammunition. Bear 3 immediately sought out the ICDC commander.

"Why don't your guards have ammunition?"

"They wasted it by shooting it in the air last night. If we give them more, they will shoot it or sell it. So we won't give them any more, they must get their own."

"Okay, but your guards don't have any ammunition. How are they supposed to stop an attack? Don't you have more ammunition in the supply room? You should have thousands of rounds."

"I am not sure, that is up to the supply officer."

After a long pause: *"Okay, let's go take a look."*

Surprisingly, the supply officer had an ample stash of ammunition all properly accounted for. It still took some convincing that it needed to be distributed though. How could a commander think it was okay for his guards not to have ammunition in their weapons? After a couple of hours of discussion and mentoring, it was finally agreed to distribute ammunition as soldiers came on shift, and then account for and collect it as they departed. Soldiers were expected to maintain one magazine of ammunition for their own personal protection, which they wouldn't have to turn in when they went off shift. Since they were at significant risk of attack as they moved to and from work, the ICDC soldiers were allowed to travel with their weapons loaded. It was also agreed that soldiers wouldn't be expected to replace ammunition themselves if they used it to defend the base or respond to enemy fire. The amount of effort and length of discussion it took just to reach these seemingly elementary decisions was mind numbing. Other surprises awaited.

During a cursory inspection of the rest of the building which now served as the ICDC headquarters (it had recently been renovated with U.S. dollars) it was discovered that all but a few of the rooms serving as offices were now filled with human feces. Apparently, despite being left with working toilettes, the Iraqi soldiers thought nothing of defecating in their own building. Worse, the ICDC leadership did nothing to prevent it. When asked about the condition of the building the Iraqis at all levels seemed unconcerned.

Bear 3 then called for an inspection of the ICDC soldiers on duty. Less than half the number required were present for duty. Not just the common soldier, but several of the Iraqi leaders were also missing. Maybe four out of twenty were in proper uniform. The same number were without ammunition. The results of the inspection were dismal, depressing and demoralizing. This was the future? This is why the U.S. Army was able to pull back from its forward bases? These were the security forces that were going to be responsible for securing the Iraqi infrastructure?

In the six plus months of working to build the ICDC in the Tarmiyah area Task Force Bear trained over 300 recruits. The highest total number of Iraqis ever actually working was closer to 200, but because of defections due to insurgent attacks and general apathy, those numbers dipped to closer to 50 by the end of February 2004. The fact that U.S. forces paid salaries in cash was an obvious enticement that kept many returning for duty, at least on payday. As the system matured and better leaders were identified, fines were levied against those soldiers who failed to show up on time, or who "lost" ammunition and weapons or committed some other offense. The fact was though that a large portion of the ICDC recruits simply stopped coming to work after milking the U.S. Army for several pay checks, an AK 47 and ammunition.

Over the next year the ICDC would morph into the Iraqi National Guard, which would then transform, by the end of 2005, into the Regular Iraqi Army. Reports of this forces' readiness to assume responsibility for security from Coalition Forces were the cause of much speculation and hope over the coming years. In fact, much of the Coalition Forces' overall strategy and transition time line were tied to expectations for the Iraqi Army's success. The reality in most of Iraq was that the ICDC and later the Iraqi Army wasn't ready to take the lead until the end of 2007 or the beginning of 2008. In places like Diyala and Baghdad where Iraqi Army and police forces were pushed to the forefront earliest, the efforts often met with calamitous, sectarian results that precipitated the violence instead of helping to control it. The ICDC, Iraqi National Guard and Iraqi Army units that became successful (and there were some) did so because they had singularly dynamic leaders with a vision for the future of Iraq; something sorely lacking in Tarmiyah in 2003-2004.

Leadership Lessons

- *Don't assume shared basic standards when dealing with another culture. Your standards may not be inherent to them.*
- *Keep expectations grounded in reality, not on hope for what the future might look like.*
- *The most important part of establishing a new organization is identifying the right leader; and they likely won't be the one most eagerly trying to impress.*

14

Operation HAMZA

THE RAID ON THE HAMZA FAMILY WAS THE CULMINATION of six months of work by Bear 2, the Task Force intelligence officer, who had pieced together vague bits of information and intelligence into a solid case for action. Saed Hamza was an influential yet inconspicuous local leader whom Bear 2 believed to be part of an insurgent network spanning the entire country. In what would emerge as an insurgent pattern, those Iraqis most involved in the early leadership of the insurgency remained largely out of view from American forces. In fact, none of the most important high-value individuals or the most significant caches of weapons or ammunition were anywhere near the places Coalition Forces regularly frequented. With few exceptions, all of TF Bear's significant successes were the result of specific intelligence painstakingly developed over hours of tactical questioning and built by cultivating positive relationships with local Iraqis. The larger cordon and search operations were often more effective for developing information and establishing local contacts than they were for producing significant captures of men or munitions.

The HAMZA operation would be a large one requiring all of the nine platoons that Task Force Bear had at its disposal. Since the departure of Bulldog Company the previous December to support the Brigade Operation to retake the city of Sammara, Task Force Bear was left with six tank platoons, one infantry platoon, a scout platoon and a mortar platoon. This was a relatively small organization of about two hundred and forty actual combat troops, tankers-scouts-infantry-field artillery, available to put into action.

Throughout the conflict in Iraq battalions, companies and platoons were often mistakenly viewed as interchangeable by higher staffs, but the reality in capabilities was sometimes striking. A tank platoon, for example, is only manned with sixteen personnel at full strength. When injuries, emergency leave and unfilled positions are taken into account, the platoon may find it difficult to man more than three combat platforms, HMMWV's or tanks, with full crews. By contrast, a full infantry platoon may have as many as thirty-six soldiers, a scout platoon thirty and some military police platoons as many as forty soldiers. A Regimental Cavalry Troop (company equivalent) will have close to a hundred and forty soldiers assigned, but a Cavalry Troop from one of the new Brigade Combat Team's Reconnaissance Squadrons has roughly seventy. Units with more soldiers obviously have more flexibility and more capability, but the reality was that battalions often got tasked the same regardless of their total strength. Delineating the discrepancies between the required tasks and the available troops to complete those tasks was one of the principle responsibilities of the battalion operations officer, in this case Bear 3. The remainder of Task Force Bear's strength, another couple of hundred soldiers, was comprised of medics and cooks and mechanics and truck drivers. All of these soldiers were required to participate in order to make the HAMZA operation possible.

Targets for the mission were broken down into three objectives with some twenty-four plus Iraqi houses and their corresponding land identified for search. The houses were numbered and prioritized. Those houses thought to contain high value targets, those identified as the most important insurgent leaders, would be raided first. Assault forces would go into these houses hard, knocking in doors with mechanical breach kits if needed. As the first houses were being entered, other forces would be establishing the outer cordon with blocking positions to prevent movement into or off of the objectives. Particular attention was given to establishing overwatch of surrounding palm groves and farmland in case anyone attempted to flee. As always, a quick reaction force, forward CP and detainee collection point as well as a rearm, refuel, recovery (R3) point would be established in a central location with easy access to all three objectives. Hit time was 0600.

Because of the number of houses and size of the areas to be searched, all Task Force soldiers were needed to conduct the mission. This meant getting approval to suspend some specified, everyday tasks and moving soldiers to positions they didn't habitually operate in. The normal counter-IED patrols on MSR Tampa would be temporarily halted. No counter-mortar OPs or patrols would be run and the QRF used for coverage on MSR Tampa would be reprioritized and relocated to better support the HAMZA operation. To free infantry and armor soldiers for the mission, cooks, medics, communications specialists and mechanics not out on the mission would assume the preponderance of force protection tasks at the patrol bases, including ECP, detainee guard and tower guard responsibilities. The bare minimum number of soldiers was left behind for these force protection duties, leaving the patrol bases at their most vulnerable to enemy attack.

Always a concern when conducting these operations was not tipping off the insurgents to the pending mission. Since the unit relied heavily on local Iraqi interpreters hired straight off the street, there was always the threat of them communicating an upcoming mission to their friends, neighbors or relatives. Even if it was inadvertent, any communication from a local Iraqi interpreter could put U.S. soldiers at risk. To mitigate this risk, interpreters were given little advanced notice of upcoming missions; most often they were simply told they were needed to spend the night. At the time it was SOP in Task Force Bear for interpreters to return home at night on non-mission days. There were no living areas for interpreters on the U.S. patrol bases, though some would remain occasionally for night-time patrolling.

By and large there were few issues with the local interpreters. They were receiving good pay, around a thousand dollars a month, and seemed to enjoy the work. Most expressed hope for their country, and while they almost universally hid their source of employment from their relatives and friends for fear of retribution, they repeatedly proved themselves loyal and courageous, even putting themselves in the line of fire during missions. It was not uncommon at the time for U.S. soldiers to outfit these local hires with weapons while on patrol, trusting them explicitly. The interpreters quickly adopted wearing U.S. uniforms, helmets and body armor when available as they assimilated into the U.S. Army culture. This also acted as a force protection measure allowing them to blend in with the patrolling unit. In retrospect the efforts of many of these "patrol terps" were truly heroic. They are certainly one of the unsung groups that contributed mightily to the U.S. successes in Iraq.

Another technique used to avoid tipping off the locals to an impending operation, was to vary the time on target. Many units fell into the rut of always conducting operations in the early morning. The most common hit time was 0200 hours. There were a couple of drawbacks to this method. First, because of the long distances from patrol bases and FOBs to most objectives, the enemy often had early warning of a raid, especially if U.S. forces were moving down a route they rarely travelled at a time they were known to conduct large operations. It became easy for local

Iraqis to discern the mission of patrol starting movement just prior to 0200 hours. Additionally, insurgent cells frequently had lookouts along the approaches to their “bed down” locations to provide early warning, often by firing off a few rounds, but sometimes using flares or simply turning lights on and off. Often the village power grid would be cut as soon as the first U.S. vehicle was seen moving into the area-an easy way to spread the alarm.

The second reason not to use 0200 as the standard hit time was that the inevitable darkness on an objective inhibited a detailed search of the surrounding area. Arriving at the objective at 0500 instead, just as it was starting to get light, was still early enough to capture most the targets, and it provided the additional benefit of a lighted search.

As the year progressed, insurgents began changing bed down locations or moving at odd times. If a target had a known business location or was suspected of moving at night, then a daylight raid may give a better chance of success. The general rule was that if the Task Force had specific intelligence tying a HVT to a place and time, then a raid was conducted at the specified time. If there was only general information about a group, family or village, a cordon and search was conducted just before sunrise in order to take advantage of the approaching daylight to assist with the search.

Patrols were also encouraged to aggressively pursue leads based on walk up sources. If a target on the Task Force HVI list was designated for capture and was identified during the course of routine operations, leaders were expected to detain him regardless of the time of day or circumstances. This led to a number of no notice raids. Platoons would transition straight from a counter-IED or security patrol into an offensive operation, often entering an Iraqi house or conducting an impromptu cordon and search. The HAMZA mission was based on good intelligence, but the exact location of the target wasn’t known, and because an all day search was anticipated the time on target was scheduled for 0600.

In the predawn light, three independent teams, each comprised of assault, security and evidence/detainee elements, moved to their objectives. A flight of two helicopters was on hand to assist in identifying any "leakers" that may attempt to flee into the refuge of nearby palm trees and farmland. Because of the lack of available routes into the area, there was no way to set a good cordon before conducting the assault. Speed and surprise by the assault force were the only ways to counter these conditions. Squads of two trucks and six to eight soldiers were dropped off from the rear of the attack column to set the outer cordon while the assault forces moved quickly ahead to the priority houses. Three to five soldiers would then go straight into the house by the most direct route while one to two others provided inner cordon security, checking back exits and courtyards.

Military age males were sequestered and questioned. Females and children would normally be grouped together in a separate room. Because operation HAMZA encompassed a large area with multiple neighborhoods, houses and families, those deemed not of interest were collected out in the front courtyards or on the street where soldiers manning the HMMWVs or BFVs could watch them. After all the houses and outbuildings were secure, teams would go back through to conduct a detailed search while tactical questioning of any persons of interest would begin.

Searches were exhaustive. Cupboards and dressers were opened. Piles of clothes were rifled through, mattresses overturned. Books and papers were examined and collected. In the outbuildings piles of debris, trash and garbage were moved to make sure they weren't concealing weapons or munitions. Barns, sheep pens and stables were inspected. Large furniture was sometimes moved to reveal secret rooms or hiding areas. Metal detectors were standard kit for all search teams. Early in the conflict, houses were often left in tatters after aggressive searches. By the time of the HAMZA operation, in early 2004, soldiers knew that everything needed to be returned to the way they had found it; thereby providing as little disruption to the local population as possible. Inevitably things did get broken. There was a claims process to repay Iraqis for damages caused by U.S. military operations. Of course when weapons or munitions were found, damages became justified.

The results of operation HAMZA were significant. In the main target house dozens of improvised rocket launchers were found, many ready to use, with additional materials and the welding equipment on hand to make scores more. The launchers were made out of angle iron with one or two strips of iron and a front and rear handle welded perpendicularly. Standard hose clamps were attached to the metal strips capable of holding rocket tubes. A simple switch tied to a nine-volt battery was then attached. Wires from the switch ran to the backside of the 57 mm rockets, which were then electrically fired. The rockets were originally intended to be fired from a rocket pod mounted to a Soviet era helicopter but were adapted for use in a direct fire mode in an around the Tarmiyah area. Firers would dip their traditional Arab headscarves in water and completely wrap their heads in order to avoid being burned by the back-blast of the rocket when fired.

In addition to being used in attacks against Task Force Bear soldiers, the launchers had also been used in attacks across Iraq. The fact that the cache was so large, that it directly implicated the number one HVT in the area and was tied to attacks in other parts of the country gave operation HAMZA the potential to have operational or even strategic significance. It was clear evidence of a supply and transportation network and implied an organizational structure to the insurgency that Coalition Forces were just starting to figure out.

Unfortunately the two priority high-value targets were

not on the objective. The raid was conducted on a Friday, the Muslim Sabbath. Task Force Bear had not properly taken the morning call to prayer into consideration when planning the timing of the mission. As a result the HVTs had departed their home roughly thirty minutes before the raid began. Through tactical questioning it was learned that the targeted individuals normally attended a mosque just a few hündred meters down the road, but the element of surprise was lost and the HVTs were gone.

As the hours of searching and detainee questioning continued, more weapons turned up. The weapons included mortar and artillery rounds, AK47s, and most importantly, a truck known to transport 57 mm rockets that Task Force Bear had been attempting to capture for two months. Several lesser high-value individuals were also detained, but strangely no 57 mm rockets to go with the launchers were found. It seemed beyond improbable that with the number of rocket launchers found and with the truck known to transport 57 mm rockets commandeered that there wouldn't be a cache of the rockets nearby. Apache Company was sent back to the highest priority house to conduct another search of the surrounding orange groves. Later, when still no rockets turned up, members of B Company were sent to search. Finally as the searches continued into their sixth hour, Bear 3 grabbed Bear 2 and went to the site himself.

The Apache Company commander met them at the site and provided a detailed description of the search techniques used. He described how they marked out and numbered a grid on the map to keep track as searches of the different areas and numbered houses were completed. In the orange grove behind the house where the rocket launchers were found, soldiers had formed a line, arms length apart, and combed the ground using metal detectors.

After a quick look around for himself, Bear 3 returned to the small clearing where Bear 2 and Apache 6 were engaged in a discussion about the implications of the ongoing operation as well as other potential search areas. A small road or trail ended in the clearing precisely where Bear 2 and Apache 6 were talking. Recent HMMWV tire marks could be seen on the trail. As Bear 3 followed the tire tracks up to the where they indicated the HMMWV had turned around he noticed a flash of blue coming out of the ground. He recognized that particular color blue from earlier cache finds; it was the color of the protective plastic end cap used on 57 mm rockets. A quick probe of the dirt uncovered a cache of over ninety rockets. A review of the earlier searches revealed why the rockets had been missed. Not only did the HMMWV tire tracks indicate that a HMMWV had conducted a three-point turn at the site of the cache, but that the HMMWV had been parked directly on top of the rockets as the soldiers had combed through the area. They had simply moved around the HMMWV, never imagining that ninety rockets were buried below a couple of inches of soil directly below the vehicle.

While the mission was a success, in a very significant way it should have been better. The key mistake was the timing of the raid. Not synchronizing the mission with the local prayer times or accounting for the fact that Saed Hamza would have to leave his home early to get to his usual mosque, resulted in a missed opportunity. Saed Hamza now knew he was being hunted and therefore would take precautions. While the physical evidence obviously indicated a more sophisticated insurgent structure than some were willing to acknowledge, without Saed Hamza to exploit for additional information, the raid was lauded for the large amount of ammunition taken off the street rather than for its wider implications.

Leadership Lessons

- *Sometimes leaders have to check themselves, especially when the facts aren't adding up to the anticipated or projected result.*

- *Failure to apply knowledge of local customs to operations will have significant implications; the emphasis on any cultural training must be how the local culture is likely to impact operations.*

15

Rocket Man

THE PHONE CALL CAME IN OVER THE SECURE PHONE at approximately 2000 hours one evening in March 2004. The mission was to conduct a cordon and search (the Army at the time had stopped calling them raids in an attempt to appear less kinetic) to capture a high value target believed responsible for the continued rocket attacks against Baghdad International Airport. The mission was tied to signals intelligence (SIGINT) that placed the target at a house deep in the countryside west of Mushaedah meaning there was a tight time window to get to the objective. Anything after 0100 hours was deemed too late to present a reasonable chance of catching the HVT. Time on target was set for 2400. The patrol of five HMMWVs and twenty-one personnel departed about two hours after receipt of the mission. The route included a forty-kilometer move with a couple of awkward turns along canal roads. If the team made the wrong turn on one of these roads, it would end up on the wrong side of the canal with no way to get across, effectively ruining any chance for surprise.

The patrol was a hodgepodge outfit with three scout gun trucks (M1025s), slick M998s and a high-back M998 for hauling human cargo. Two of the 1025s were from the scout platoon. It included the scout platoon leader and eight of his scouts. Another M1025 and the high-back M998 were from the mortar platoon. The remaining vehicle, a "slick" M998, carried the command and control element that included, Bear 3, Bear 2 and the category two interpreter (meaning he was vetted for a security clearance). None of the vehicles were up-armored save for some sheet metal half doors on the command and control vehicle with sandbags added to the floor for protection from an IED detonation from under the vehicle. While this was a non-standard team for this type of mission, it was not an unusual combination of forces for Task Force Bear. In fact cobbling together combat power for short notice missions became the norm due to the brutal troops to task shortage. Task Force Bear as with most battalion sized combat units in 2003-2004 needed another company or two to ensure enough combat power to execute these types of short notice, high priority missions while simultaneously conducting its other specified tasks.

The target information was passed from the special operations forces through the Brigade HQ to Task Force Bear. This immediately caused the Task Force leadership to suspect its accuracy, timeliness and importance. After nine months conducting counterinsurgency operations in Iraq none of the missions generated from higher headquarters panned out as advertised. The thinking went that if the special operations task force had really believed in the accuracy of the intelligence and the importance of the targeted individual, they would have executed the mission themselves. Fortunately, the mission packet for this operation was detailed. It included imagery of two suspected houses; a primary and alternate objective, and was based on very recent and confirmed intelligence passed from national assets. In the short amount of time given to prepare for the operation, it was determined there wasn't enough combat power available to hit both objectives simultaneously. During planning only the primary objective was discussed.

The target was the purported leader of the anti-Iraqi forces (AIF) cell responsible for shooting rockets into

Baghdad International Airport. Despite many “dry holes” from similar types of short notice missions based on obscure intelligence sources in the past, all the soldiers and leaders were eager and amped as they departed for the mission. There were only two weeks left before Task Force Bear redeployed from Iraq. This would be one of the final missions and there was always the chance it would be an important one.

A scout weapons team of two OH58D helicopters would link up in route to help secure the objective while a patrol from Apache Company would remain on standby at a coordination point along MSR Tampa to provide a QRF in case the team got into trouble. As Bear 3 locked and loaded rolling out the gate from forward operating base (FOB) Bear, he shouted to Bear 2 over his shoulder “what do you think?”

“I don’t know. It all depends on how good the intel is.”

“Well, at least it should be a quick one. He’ll either be there or he won’t and we’ll be home by 0200 easy.”

The helicopters arrived when the patrol was still 5 kilometers from the objective. The HMMWVs moved slowly because the canal roads were tight. It was difficult work matching the overhead imagery picture of a house to reality on the ground. Bear 3 was relying heavily on his GPS. It was about 2300, fortunately the moon was good.

“Bear 3, Bear 3, this is Night Stalker 2-0,” the helicopters reporting in.

“This is Bear 3, we’re still about 10-15 minutes out, break... I need you to hold vicinity check point 3 until we hit the release point. Over.”

Bear 3 wanted to keep the helicopters out of audible range of the objective because helicopters flying nearby often alerted locals to pending operations.

“Roger that. We’ll move to check point 3 and wait for your call.”

“Roger. What is your weapons configuration and how much time do you have on station?”

"This is Night Stalker 2-0. We have a mix of rockets and fifty cal... We have a little over an hour before we need to break for gas."

"This is Bear 3. Roger; I'll give you a call when we're at the RP... would like you to orient south of the main house and keep anyone from moving through the fields, break; we'll be moving south from the canal road... We've got five trucks and will be marked with infra-red chemlights."

"This is Night Stalker 2-0, roger that... what are the engagement criteria if someone is leaving the house."

"This is supposedly a known bad guy, break... if you see someone running out the back attempt to shoot a warning shot, break... but if you need to... consider hostile and engage. Over."

"This is Night Stalker 2-0, WILCO."

"Thanks. Out."

These aircrews had been working with Task Force Bear steadily for months and it was normally possible to recognize individuals from their voice on the radio. Recognizing a pilot's voice gave soldiers on the ground a lot of confidence. The aircraft greatly improved security for the ground unit especially because this was a hasty mission executed without a full rehearsal or detailed reconnaissance.

The patrol halted briefly at a point where two canals and several roads intersected. The lead scout wanted to take the route moving due west. Others wanted to move southwest along the southern edge of a smaller canal. During mission analysis the best route was identified, but now on the ground it was not so clear. The battalion rarely used this route. Few had been on it when conducting the initial area reconnaissance; others had used it once to egress from an objective a couple of months earlier. Both routes led past the target house, but one would leave the assault force on the wrong side of a canal, with no way to cross for 20 kilometers. Time was growing short and the aircraft had a limited station time. They moved to the southwest and told themselves this looked like the right way. Several minutes later…

"Night Stalker 2-0 this is Bear 3. We are at the RP. Move now."

"The is Night Stalker 2-0. Roger."

"Stalker 1, that's the house... That's the house."

The lead HMMWV raced forward to the edge of the compound wall and turned south down an alley to establish part of the outer cordon. Soldiers spilled out of the next HMMWV before it had fully stopped and rushed toward the house. The C2 HMMWV and HMMWV numbers four and five also stopped in front of the objective house. Soldiers disembarked and took up positions. Some soldiers were designated as security and stayed outside of the house, covering window and doors. The assault team (five soldiers) opened the main door to the house (the doors were rarely locked) and quickly entered. The final HMMWV stopped short of the objective; orienting their .50 caliber machinegun back down the ingress route. The aircraft arrived over the objective area.

"Bear 3 this is Night Stalker 2-0."

"This is Bear 3. We're on the objective with friendlies inside the house. Do you have eyes to the south?"

"Affirmative, Bear 3."

"Roger. Out."

This was close to the sixtieth preplanned, named operation the battalion was executing. Task force Bear soldiers had entered literally hundreds of houses over the past nine months; none had drawn contact.

The occupants of the house were taken by surprise. In the house, there were six to eight adult males socializing in the house's main meeting room. Bear 2 went to work questioning the Iraqis as the rest of the soldiers secured the house and began to search the outbuildings. Women and children were sequestered in their own room. They would be questioned in time.

The owner of the house, Saed Habib, didn't match the description of the HVT Task Force Bear was looking for. He was, however, in possession of a satellite phone which automatically made him suspect. In 2004 there were almost zero cell phones in Iraq, and satellite phones were a rarity held mostly by high-level Iraqi Government Officials, contractors or insurgents. When questioned about the SATPHONE Habib revealed that he had borrowed it from a friend in order to make a call outside the country to some relatives. This friend, according to Habib, traveled regularly to and from Baghdad and was involved in international business. After some additional questioning by Bear 2 Habib suddenly and unexpectedly offered that his friend happened to be staying in a house nearby. Quickly conferring with each other and checking imagery Bear 2 determined that the house Habib was describing was actually the secondary objective passed to Task Force Bear as part of the original intelligence dump. Better yet, Habib volunteered to lead the team directly to the house. Unfortunately, although the house was less than five kilometers away, a bridge along the only direct route had been damaged and was closed to vehicular traffic. (it was later realized this had been done intentionally to limit access by Coalition Forces to the area)

Habib claimed to know of an alternate route and agreed to show the way as a passenger in the Team's lead HMMWVs. Since no contraband was discovered on the first objective, the team mounted up and headed toward the second objective. The time was approximately 0130 hours. Just as they were leaving they got a call from Night Stalker two zero.

"Bear 3, this is Night Stalker 2-0."

"This is Bear 3."

"This is Night Stalker 2-0. We are out of gas and need to return to base. Are you going to need us back out here?"

"This is Bear 3. Negative, Night Stalker 2-0. Thanks for the help."

"This is Night Stalker 2-0. Be safe."

It was a calculated risk. Bringing the helicopters back would provide much needed firepower, observation and deterrence to any planned attack. But Bear 3 was concerned that helicopters moving in support might alert any nearby insurgents that U.S. forces were still operating in the area. Since he didn't know exactly where Habib was taking them he didn't want to chance that the helicopters would inadvertently fly over the target house and alert those inside. Better to move quietly, with no lights, and count on the element of surprise to give them the best chance of success.

Moving down dirt roads, flanked by canals, at night without the aid of lights was methodical. No one on the Team really knew where the Iraqi source, Habib, was leading them. Was it a trap? Was there an ambush waiting for them on the other end? The fact that Habib willingly rode in the lead vehicle gave the Team some measure of confidence that there wasn't an IED around the next bend. When a civilian vehicle approached from the opposite direction, however, everyone became wary. Was it a coincidence that a civilian vehicle was on the road, the only apparent route between the two objectives, at near 0200 in the morning with four adult males inside the vehicle? Compounding the suspicion was the fact that members of the Team had seen this car and driver before. Shortly after the raid commenced, this exact driver and car approached one of the blocking positions. He and several family members in the car with him were questioned and casually searched. After finding nothing suspicious, they were turned around and sent on their way. Now this car and driver had returned, but instead of his wife and children, the driver was transporting three adult males. One learns early on not to believe in coincidences in Iraq. It was worth stopping to question the individuals. Maybe one of them was the HVT.

Since the man driving the car was supposedly a local,

the hastily developed plan called for using the informant, Saed Habib, to confirm his identity and hopefully the identity of the remaining males. Habib would stay seated in the HMMWV with a scarf around his head concealing his identity. The passengers in the car would be brought forward one a time with a flashlight shining into their eyes to keep them from seeing who was observing them. Habib promptly identified the four men; Jabar-Ahmed-Mohamed, Abdulla-Ahmed-Mohamed, Hatim-Kareem-Mohamed and Jamal-Kathem-Mohamed. According to traditional Arabic naming conventions the first two were brothers because they shared their father's name (Ahmed) and grandfather's name (Mohamed). All were potentially cousins as they all had shared at least the third name (Mohamed). Habib confirmed this, additionally stating that he knew the four individuals well as they all occupied farms nearby. Once this base line of information was established, each of the men from the car were questioned independently. The first three gave stories that all matched the information provided by Habib. The fourth individual, however, denied knowing any of the other three. He claimed to be hitch hiking from Baghdad when the others picked him up, agreeing to allow him to spend the night at their home out of charity. This made no sense. The source, Habib, and the three other men all independently corroborated each other's story. Either this was a well thought out and rehearsed ruse or someone wasn't telling the truth. All evidence pointed to the latter.

For his part the fourth individual, Jamal, adamantly stuck with his original story. Even when told of the others cooperation and the information they provided he would not recant. This was taking too much time! Now after 0200 the patrol was losing its momentum and perhaps its initiative. Bear 3 had had enough. Approaching Jamal Bear 3 explained that unless he could somehow unravel the discrepancies between the two versions of events he would have no choice, but to detain Jamal and take him back to the American patrol base. Inexplicably Jamal didn't budge.

Why was this so hard? Jamal was loaded into the back of the cargo HMMWV for transportation back to the Task Force detention facility where he would be questioned in more depth. In the meantime, he was rewarded by having to accompany the assault force onto the next objective.

Now approaching 0230 hours the patrol continued movement. The route Habib took them on was outside the normal operating area of Task Force Bear. Radio traffic was spotty.

"Apache White 1 [Apache's QRF], this is Bear 3."

Silence.

"Bear X-ray, this is Bear 3. Over."

Silence.

"Any Apache, any Apache element? This is Bear 3. Over."

Finally a weak transmission: "*This is Apache QRF. Over.*"

"This is Bear 3. Relay to Bear X-ray. Break. We are continuing our move to the second objective vicinity grid mike-sierra-one-five-seven-two, seven-five-three-two; I say again: We are moving to the secondary objective; we now have one detainee."

"This is Apache White One. Roger. Over."

There was more to the transmission, but the only sound heard was static, they were officially outside communications distance from any supporting forces

Movement continued tentatively. The patrol was being directed by an unknown source along an unknown set of roads, out of radio contact, to an objective that was assumed to be the one on the imagery but without any real hint at what would be found there. There was no helicopter support and no way to get in touch with any element in case of attack or casualties. Bear 6 had made it clear over the radio before the team departed the primary objective that they did not have to continue to the next objective if they felt the risk was too great. In the original task the second objective was not deemed essential. Faced with what was perhaps their last combat mission in Iraq, and disappointed with the results so far, the decision was easy. They would go for it.

Several hundred meters out from what was thought to be the second objective, the patrol came to a narrow bridge. The HMMWVs with their wide wheelbase would barely fit across after a tight turn. Dismounts quickly jumped out of the HMMWVs to ground guide vehicles one by one over the bridge. The delay caused a slight break in the patrol as drivers struggled to get the HMMWVs across the bridge. This resulted in a gap in the patrol with the two lead vehicles getting out in front of Bear 3 by a couple hundred meters.

"Stalker 1, this is Bear 3. Slow your move."

"This is Stalker 1. We're dismounting now!"

The lead vehicles of the patrol had come up on the second objective more quickly than anticipated. When the source finally told them to stop they were directly in front of the target house. Fearing that the noise of the HMMWVs would alert anyone in the house Stalker 1 didn't hesitate, grabbing three other soldiers he rushed through the front door. Bear 3 and Bear 2 catching up with their HMMWV after being delayed at the bridge arrived just after the lead team entered the house. Bear 3 sprang from his vehicle with Bear 2 and their CAT 2 interpreter, Ahmed, in tow. Recognizing that Stalker 1 had entered through the front door and that the remaining two HMMWVs were still navigating the bridge Bear 3 detoured around to the rear of the house to provide security and prevent any escape.

Shouting erupted from inside. On his way into the house, Bear 2 stopped at a van that was up on jacks blocking the front gate to the courtyard of the house. He pulled open the door, 9mm pistol drawn, expecting to clear the van before moving on. What he found gave him the fright of his life. There were two young men with AK 47s inside the van. Apparent lookouts who had either fallen asleep or been paralyzed by fear at the unexpected arrival of American troops at 0300 in the morning. Bear 2 quickly charged his weapon. He would later receive much ribbing for moving onto an objective without a round in the chamber. Fortunately, the enemy failed to defend themselves. Another close call averted

Out back Bear 3 made a quick check of the perimeter. No obvious exit points from the main house. He could hear the team on the inside as it cleared from room to room. He noticed a light coming from under a door to an outbuilding attached to a storage shed. Moving at an oblique angle to the door, he knocked hard. He heard noises from inside. A short time later the door opened. A man appeared in dishdasha (the traditional Arab tunic) and black beard. Bear 3 motioned the man back, cursing internally that he hadn't learned more Arabic. The man backed through a short room to stand next to a woman and small boy. Nervously Bear 3 stepped through the doorway. The outbuilding consisted of a storage room, a kitchen and a bedroom. A shotgun leaned against a wall. It appeared to Bear 3 that he must have woken them up.

The outbuilding was so much smaller and less elegant than the facade of the main home. Bear 3 assumed this must be a caretaker and his family. He backed out of the building, keeping his M4 at the high ready oriented at the adult male.

"I've got people out back," he shouted. *"Send some security around back."*

This all took place in just a couple of minutes. Shortly afterwards the remaining trucks arrived on the objective. American soldiers hustled to set security to the rear of the building and relieve Bear 3 of his guard duty. Now he could get inside and find out what was going on.

"The Target is not here," Bear 2 blurted out as Bear 3 entered the building.

"At least no one matching that description."

"What do we have?"

"About eight males all sleeping down here in the main

room; one guy upstairs in bed with his wife, a bunch of computers, and get this. Ahmer says these guys aren't Iraqi."

"What do you mean?"

"They don't speak with Iraqi accents. He noticed it right away."

Just then Ahmer starts yelling and cursing at one of the men in Arabic, he slaps one repeatedly.

"Ahmer, what are you doing? Hey, get him out of here."

"Sir, you don't understand, these guys aren't Iraqi; that one is Moroccan that one is Syrian. What are they doing in Iraq? They have no business here."

"How do you know?"

"They don't speak like Iraqis. Their Arabic is different, its easy to tell they aren't from here."

"Okay, let's round them up, I don't want to be on the objective long."

"A U.S. soldier runs in from outside."

"Sir, we've got weapons out back."

"What kind?"

"Machine guns, AK47s, RPGs, it's a big haul."

"Let's go look."

"Oh, I forgot to tell you Bear 2; there is a guy and his family in the outbuilding; looks like a caretaker, probably need to talk to him."

Bear 2, Bear 3 and Ahmer moved to the backyard. It was indeed a large cache. Perhaps more importantly, the weapons were all in ready conditions; well oiled and loaded. Better yet, the man Bear 3 assumed was a likely caretaker was identified by Bear 2 as the HVT. JACKPOT!

The results of the raid were significant. Weapons were taken off the street. The man most likely responsible for the rocket attacks against Baghdad International Airport detained. Most importantly, a cell of foreign fighters was disrupted. At this point in the war there was a lot of anecdotal evidence of foreign fighters being used to amplify the insurgency, but there was very little hard evidence. Now there was a group of twelve men, linked to weapons and a known attacker, not to mention the bevy of information to be harvested from the computers. As far as Task Force Bear knew this was the first capture of foreign fighters in Multi Division North's area of operation. This could be a capture with operational and even strategic implications. Now the only problem was getting them back to base.

Including the informant, Habib, from the first objective and the Iraqi picked up along the way from the car, the assault team now had fourteen detainees. There was a lot of banter on the objective about what to do with the informant. The fear was that if released he would most likely be killed. There would be no question in the local community as to who led the Americans to the foreign fighter house. At the same time he was not viewed as a threat and there was sentiment that he should be rewarded for helping U.S. forces when they otherwise would have been at a dead end. When asked, the informant himself seemed ambivalent to being returned to his home or being detained. As 4 A.M. approached it was decided to include him in with the other detainees. Hopefully this would take some suspicion off of him. He could always be released later if he proved innocent. And there was always the chance that he knew more than he was letting on.

With fourteen detainees stuffed in the back of the high-back cargo HMMWV there was not room to transport the large quantity of weapons. The decision was made to take the weapons back to base using the flatbed civilian truck seized from the objective. It was easy to find a volunteer from among the U.S. soldiers to drive the truck. The soldier would only incur a slightly increased risk of getting hurt in an attack, since none of the HMMWVs were armored anyway. In some respects, the soldier driving the civilian truck was less likely to be hit with an IED or ambush because any attacker would focus on the American vehicles.

As the evidence was sorted and loaded for transport, the CAT 2 interpreter, Ahmer, was once again berating the captured foreigners. When the detainees were not as contrite as he demanded, Ahmer became incensed; lashing out with words and threatening kicks and slaps.

*"Get him away from the f***ing detainees!"*

For a man who had been away from Iraq for thirteen years he was certainly passionate about the meddling by foreigners in the future of Iraq. In his mind they had no justification for Jihad and their mere presence in Iraq proved their guilt. This belief was one shared throughout Iraq. Regardless of political or religious persuasion there was almost universal disdain among Iraqis for all outsiders, not just U.S. soldiers but Saudis and Moroccans and Egyptians. There was no place for foreigners in Iraq and no reason for them to be there.

Iraqis are certainly proud people and they do have a vision for a unified, prosperous and strong country. Unfortunately, the vision is different among each ethnic and religious group. The Kurdish vision for Iraq includes a sovereign Kurdish land as part of a loose confederation. The Sunnis feel it is their birthright to administer Iraq from a strong central government controlling the natural resources and acting as a check against aggressive Persian influence. The religious and secular Shia have different goals, but they all include closer relations with Iran than the Sunni desire and feature the Shia majority in firm control of the key military and financial positions of power. At one point a prominent Shia faction also preferred to go the confederation route, with the idea of a homogenous southern Shia state with strong Iranian ties. This group was defeated during internal Shia on Shia fighting in the mid years of the conflict. In any event the visceral reaction of Ahmer to the foreign fighters found on the objective, by an otherwise quiet and passive man, was an important lesson about how ardent even Iraqi ex-patriots were about the future of Iraq and the ubiquitous disdain for foreigners.

Back on the objective there was no good way to fit fourteen detainees into the back of a cargo HMMWV. When the mission started Bear 3 was expecting one or two detainees, certainly not fourteen. The detainees were flex-cuffed, blindfolded and literally stacked on top of each other. The route back was pockmarked with potholes and broken asphalt, a rough ride. If the late night travelling conditions, down unfamiliar roads, made the U.S. soldiers wary and eager to get back to base, the detainees were terrified. At least one defecated himself and another pissed himself. About a quarter of the way back several of them started screaming. The patrol pulled over to check on them and found a pile of tangled legs, arms, piss and feces. Their legs and arms were going numb from lack of circulation because of the tight and awkward conditions. The detainees were quickly shuffled and the patrol continued its move, arriving back at FOB Bear without further incident.

Within hours of returning the news of the capture of foreign fighters had worked its way up the chain. Later that day two special operations helicopters flew in to pick up the detainees, computers and other evidence. Task Force Bear also sent forces back to the objective to conduct a more detailed, daylight search and after operations reconnaissance. No additional weapons, munitions or evidence was found. It's unclear what ever happened to that particular group of foreigners. Task Force Bear departed Iraq a short time later, and no report ever made it back to the leadership on the results of the interrogation or evidence exploitation. The capture of the foreign fighter cell just before the redeployment was a satisfying last operation. For a Tank Battalion Task Force, conducting a dismounted raid, at night, with a cobbled together group of soldiers and less than perfect situational awareness, the success of the mission proved the acme of Task Force Bear's performance. During the unit's first mission (see chapter 2) it had been relegated to a secondary objective by the special operations forces. It took most of the battalion to conduct the operation and a gaffe at the SP almost derailed the entire mission. The assault force missed the turn to its objective three times and then entered the wrong house, despite having detailed information on its location. When the Task Force returned to the attack position, they were ambushed because they hadn't properly secured the area; and then, failed to return fire.

The success of this final operation, with less than two hours to plan, across much more difficult terrain and dependent on developing and exploiting intelligence on the fly showed that Task Force Bear was a learning organization that had mastered its craft. Unfortunately Task Force Bear was about to be sent home where its leadership would disperse to fill other positions across the Army. Other units, new and inexperienced units would deploy to take its place.

Leadership Lessons

- *Success may require doing more than the original task-stay focused on the purpose of the mission.*
- *Leaders are required to weigh risks to potential gain. Don't expect success without having to take risk. Prepare for it.*

Conclusions: Counterinsurgency

IT WAS RECOGNIZED BY MANY EARLY IN THE CONFLICT THAT the Iraqi people were the key to success, the center of gravity, in Iraq. The United States could be successful only after co-opting the Iraqi people to its cause. Senior U.S. Army leaders were saying as early as 2003 that there was no military solution to the problems in Iraq. A recognition that military force alone could not co-opt the Iraqi people. The fact that this was understood so early should not be surprising. In every type of warfare it is generally accepted that to achieve victory the will of the opposing nation must be broken. Nothing embodies the will of a nation but its people, either the whole population or its controlling factions.

At the beginning of the conflict the average Iraqi had but two choices: support one of the factions of the insurgency, or support the U.S. Army. For the proud Arab, this was an easy decision. Culturally, historically they would oppose the invader. The fact that the United States Army was not welcomed as a liberating force surprised many and belied one of the central pre-invasion assumptions— that Iraqis wanted a chance to chose their system of government and when given the choice would chose to embrace the Western model. When these assumptions proved false, soldiers and leaders quickly realized they had a lot to learn about the Iraqi people and culture before they could even begin to start solving the tactical problems facing them.

Since the people were the center of gravity; providing for their needs should have been the first priority. Providing for a person's needs also implies an understanding of their condition and their culture. Abraham Maslow, in his 1943 paper *A Theory of Human Motivation*, teaches that the population's first needs are food, water and shelter; followed by security. Food, water and shelter were never wide spread problems in Iraq. Most people were making do as they had before the U.S. invasion. What *had* changed most significantly was their security situation along with the expectation that things would immediately get better with the arrival of the Americans. Gone was the Iraqi state apparatus that, while commonly brutal, at least provided some kind of structure and rules, a point of departure from which to live. Without this structure the insurgents adopted the guise of religious organizations and political parties in an attempt to fill the vacuum. They promised security through participation in and acceptance of various religious dogmas and militias. This led to the rise of leaders like Muqtada al Sadr and his Mehdi Militia as well as the initial acceptance of organizations like Al Qaeda-Iraq.

The Coalition Forces did not have well developed or articulated alternatives to offer. They had not secured the country in the immediate wake of victory, had disbanded the only indigenous security force, the Iraqi Army, and from early on made it clear that it was looking to leave Iraq at the earliest opportunity. The number of troops in Iraq were not sufficient for units such as Task Force Bear to secure places like Tarmiyah; not to mention Baghdad, Mosul, Falujah, Ramadi, Najaf, Baquba or Samarra. This dearth of troops continued until the "surge" of 2007 and was aided greatly by the rising capabilities of Iraq's own Army and Police as well as the Sunni Awakening or "Sahwa" initiative.

The only way to have ensured the proper number of troops for the task at hand was to have developed a clearly articulated vision and well defined end-state. Without a vision and endstate there is no real way to match capabilities against requirements, or to determine shortfalls. When no weapons of mass destruction were found and after Saddam Hussein was captured, a new objective was needed to focus the efforts of Coalition Forces. Brigades and divisions struggled to delineate decisive operations and main efforts. Battalions were left largely to figure it out as they went along. Soldiers and leaders at all levels and units of all sizes were doing a lot of work, but it was all method. Leaders started talking about "advancing the football" instead of talking about how to achieve victory.

The football metaphor is a prescient one. Unfortunately, American soldiers, leaders and units were attempting to advance a football not realizing that the dimensions of the field had changed, that the opposing team didn't wear uniforms, that the ball weighed twenty kilograms, that there were no referees and neither side knew the rules of the game; the insurgents were not playing football at all.

Determining and communicating a clear vision and defining a measurable end-state require one thing above all else: leadership. If leaders are struggling to provide vision and endstate it is an indication that the problem being addressed is not properly understood. This is especially true when fighting a counterinsurgency. Vision and endstate must not only be communicated to friendly forces, but more importantly must be communicated to and understood by the local population and the formal and informal indigenous brokers of power.

Conclusions: Organizational Leadership

THE EVENTS PORTRAYED IN THE PRECEDING CHAPTERS illustrate a small portion of the diverse challenges confronted by organizational leaders in Iraq. The leadership lessons derived from these events illuminate recurring themes that should have relevance beyond military organizations and military problems. These themes can generally be grouped into six areas.

1. *Consideration and understanding of second and third order effects (consequences).*
2. *Understanding the operational environment and how it affects what you want to accomplish (i.e. know the people and culture you are trying to influence).*
3. *Accounting for, incorporating and synchronizing other organizations that influence your battlespace.*
4. *Communicating vision and endstate.*
5. *Underwriting acceptable risk and mitigating unacceptable risk.*
6. *Taking direct action (applying direct leadership) when needed.*

The first three areas are inter-related and must be addressed by leaders proactively. Meaning leaders must prepare their organizations to be proficient in them before the start of operations. It is not enough for the organizational leader to be a subject matter expert. The challenge is how to make these competencies part of organizational culture. The leader is still responsible to ensure his organization understands its environment, incorporates and accounts for subordinate and peripheral units and considers second and third order consequences, but the leader cannot and should not perform these tasks exclusively.

Consideration of second and third order effects must be ingrained as part of the staff planning process. Understanding the indigenous peoples and cultures must be ingrained at all levels of the organization to accurately gauge second and third order effects and to maximize potential influence over the population. Accounting for and synchronizing the effects of other organizations that influence the area of responsibility depends on strong organizational standard operating procedures and a clear dialogue about expectations and guidelines. The organizational leader certainly could (and should) be a part of this process, but should never be the single point of success or failure.

Addressing the last three areas are the essence of organizational leadership and are where the organizational leader should focus most of his or her efforts. Communicating vision and endstate may be *the* essential element. While there is no universally accepted definition of organizational leadership, nearly all definitions stress the need for the leader to communicate a clear direction. In the Army this is called the commander's vision and endstate (also called intent). The endstate provides the objective and the vision provides guidelines on how to achieve the objective. The Army states that "…organizational leaders must be able to translate complex concepts into understandable operational and tactical plans and decisive action." (Army Field Manual 6-22, October 2006, p 1-11) Business and academic literature on organizational leadership approach the definition from a different perspective but also recognize the necessity for an understandable and succinct description of the direction and goals of the organization. In his book *Leading Change*, Harvard Business School Professor John Kotter writes that "without an appropriate vision, a transformation effort can easily dissolve into a list of confusing, incompatible, and time-consuming projects that go in the wrong direction or nowhere at all."

In Iraq articulating vision and endstate proved elusive. It was easier to focus on the metrics used to gauge progress. Many leaders became focused on the number of attacks, number of enemy killed or captured, number of artillery rounds fired, number of patrols conducted and/or the number of U.S. casualties. These areas certainly deserved attention, but not at the expense of a clearly articulated vision and endstate. Too often early in the Iraq conflict leaders defaulted to what they were comfortable with. The result was almost four years of ambiguous messages that mid level leaders struggled to translate into appropriate actions on the ground.

The lack of an acute vision and endstate from higher HQ impacted all of Task Force Bear's long-range decisions and plans. Not knowing if the priority of operations was enemy focused (kill and capture bad guys), population focused (secure the population), Iraqi government focused (establish the institutions of government and infrastructure) or force protection focused (limit the number of U.S. casualties) inhibited the ability to maximize effects. As a result, different units operating next to and sometimes through each other's battlespace were as likely to desynchronize operations as they were to complement operations. The failure to synchronize the military and political boundaries surrounding the Tarmiya Qadah is a significant example of lack of vision that produced long-term consequences. (See Chapter 10.) Closing Patrol Base Animal to reduce U.S. interaction with local Iraqis is another.

Underwriting acceptable risk— i.e letting subordinates leaders know what risks are acceptable in the pursuit of an endstate, as well as mitigating unacceptable risk— i.e risks that you don't want your subordinates to take on their own, is another essential element of organizational leadership. Too often leaders were second-guessed after their actions disrupted the efforts of a higher HQ or had an operational or strategic impact. This was especially true if the actions resulted in U.S. casualties. Occasionally this second-guessing was warranted, but frequently units and leaders were censured for the consequences of too many tasks, too few troops and an inadequate vision and endstate linking requirements and capabilities to an achievable objective.

The operation outlined in chapter fifteen illustrates what can happen when leaders effectively underwrite risk. Before heading out on the short notice mission in search of "rocket man", Bear 6 gave Bear 3 the authority to make the call about moving to the secondary objective. This authority gave Bear 3 the confidence to continue to the second objective even though the route took him outside communications range and outside the Task Force's normal operating area. Each of these conditions normally would have caused cancellation of the mission. But because leaders had discussed the risks in relation to the potential reward and took into account the context of the operational environment at that time and place, Bear 3 continued the mission to a successful conclusion.

Exercising direct leadership must always be an option for the organizational leader. All leaders must identify the point of command they need to position themselves at to best influence the entire organization and the outcome of the mission. Organizational leaders uncomfortable taking direct action when needed should be relegated to leading small groups accomplishing banal tasks. The problem in the Army is more often than not the opposite. Army leaders spend all of their early careers as direct leaders. They are taught and expected to lead from the front and be the technical and tactical expert. Direct leaders who fail to recognize their transition to organizational leadership often default to their earlier comfort zones. These leaders spend their time rushing to contact or quizzing subordinates on technical solutions instead of looking forward in anticipation of transitions or new challenges.

The early experiences of Task Force Bear provide numerous examples of organizational leaders necessarily applying direct leadership. The poor response of the Task Force to initial contact in chapter one was unacceptable. If the unit continued operating in that way there is no doubt it would have sustained significantly more casualties and been ineffective at accomplishing its mission. Fortunately, through training, repetition and articulating the right and left limits of acceptable risk at the appropriate level, junior leaders became more aggressive taking initiative. This allowed Task Force Bear to grow as an organization. From a unit that failed to respond to enemy fire in chapter one, to being capable of conducting a short notice raid, at night, outside of radio contact and the normal operating area of the unit. It also allowed the Task Force Bear organizational leaders to focus on long -term effects and synchronization of efforts instead of being constantly drawn in to fixing short range problems.

Great organizational leaders must be anticipatory. They must be able to project the consequences of any chosen action or inaction. They must be able to understand the second and third order effects of a decision and be able to live with those effects when they don't turn out as expected. A good leader has the courage to take risks. A great organizational leader has the judgment to know which risks are appropriate to take and when, and how best to recover when those risks inevitably cause events to go awry.

As hopefully evidenced by the preceding chapters, the battalions, companies, platoons and soldiers fighting in Iraq were trained and flexible enough to grow, learn and adapt as organizations. This organizational growth didn't just happen. It was continuously sought and encouraged by leaders from within the organizations themselves. Despite these efforts there were certainly inconsistencies and tragedies over the course of the conflict. There were mistakes made at all levels. It is still true that warfare by its nature is messy business.

By internalizing and institutionalizing the organizational leadership lessons learned from the conflict in Iraq, namely; anticipating second and third order effects, understanding how local culture impacts operations, synchronizing the efforts of related organizations, accounting for risk, taking direct action when needed and most importantly communicating a clear vision and endstate, organizational leaders should be better prepared to meet the challenges of coming conflicts.

In any case, the decisive factor for success in war (or I would argue for success solving any organizational problem) will not change regardless of the complexities of future conflicts. That decisive factor, recognized as the most important element of combat power, the hallmark of every great nation, army and organization, is good leadership.

Afterward

THERE ARE MANY MORE LESSONS TO LEARN ABOUT leadership and counterinsurgency tactics, techniques and procedures. There are also many areas that weren't addressed in enough detail by this book. Areas like civil affairs and state department efforts to build civil and economic capacity, development of the Iraqi Police, the Sons of Iraq program, infrastructure development, and the national and provincial elections were all significant initiatives deserving more discussion. The struggle by Coalition Forces to establish any kind of relevant information operations cannot be underestimated and alone should be the subject of additional writings. Certainly an organizational level discussion on how to deal with morale problems resulting from death and injury would be worthy of additional writing. The role of the organizational leader in motivating or inspiring his unit was also not discussed. While many of these areas played some role in Task Force Bear's counterinsurgency activities in 2003 and early 2004, they were not the critical areas they later became. It will be left to another book, and perhaps other authors, to address these significant omissions.

Epilogue

I AM SOMETIMES ASKED HOW I FEEL ABOUT MY TIME in Iraq now that it is known that the reasons we were committed to war, the availability of weapons of mass destruction and the implication of terrorist associations by Saddam Hussein, were proven false. I offer to those who pose this question the following for consideration:

How does this question matter to the soldier on the ground in Iraq? Does it help him stay alive? Does it help him keep his buddy alive? Does it help him accomplish his mission? Does it help him treat Iraqi civilians with respect? Does it help him treat others as he wishes to be treated? Can the power of a nation be sustained by a volunteer military that questions the decisions its leaders make? Would it help the situation to become a conscientious objector? Or refuse to deploy? Or resign from the Army? Or not reenlist? Would that make our Nation stronger?

The fact is we *are* in Iraq (and Afghanistan), following the orders of our elected President, in a war that both houses of Congress voted to support and have voted to continue funding. Despite political infighting, the mistakes, bad policies, the gnashing of teeth and political wrangling, the Nation should be proud of its Army and its soldiers. They have preformed remarkably under very difficult circumstances.

Imagine yourself… in a strange, far away land, where problems have no recognizable solutions; where few hope for your success and many openly oppose you; where every sight, sound, taste and smell is different; where no one speaks your language; where death is a more normal part of life; where native honor means taking care of family at the expense of the truth; where history and experience tells the population to resist the foreigner; where religion is used by those in power to bend the people to their will; where young men get paid for throwing bombs at you, and get paid even more if they kill you; where graft and nepotism are expected and accepted as part of the system; where kindness and charity are viewed as naiveté and weakness; where a people who are used to having nothing see what you have and want more; where you are always wondering if the person you are speaking with wants to kill you.

So I offer a simple answer to those who may pose the previous question.

It doesn't matter, I've done my duty, the job I swore an oath to do. I've made mistakes. Certainly there are things I wish I had done better, but at the end of the day I have done my best and focused on the *solution* instead of the problem.

The more important question may be to those who would pose such questions to American soldiers is…

What have you done?

Glossary of Terms and Acronyms

"A Team" .... Operational Detachment Alpha; a 10-12 man special forces detachment

AAR .... After actions review; introspective process to figure out how to do the job better next time

AK 47 .... Soviet era automatic rifle

AOR .... Area of Responsibility; a unit is responsible for everything that happens inside its area of responsibility, normally marked by Military boundaries

AQI .... Al Qaeda Iraq

AWT .... Air Weapons Team

AH64 .... Apache "attack" helicopter

BDA .... Battle Damage Assessment

Battle Drill Six.......... The collective task to enter and clear a room, normally performed by a dismounted team of 3-5 soldiers

Battlespace................ The area where combat operations may take place; see also AOR

Bradley .... See BFV

BFT .... Blue Force Tracker; a device that allows military vehicles to display map information and share text messages

BFV .... Bradley Fighting Vehicle; see M2 and Infantry Fighting Vehicle
BN .... Battalion
CP .... Check point
C2 .... Command and control; normally comprised of leadership and communications elements
ECP .... Entry control point
EFP .... Explosively formed projective; a particularly dangerous type of IED
FBCB2 .... Future Battle Command Brigade and Below; and encrypted version of BFT
FOB .... Forward operating base; major base where U.S. soldiers lived in Iraq
Handmikes .... Hand held microphones that let you talk and hear over a radio
HMMWV .... High Mobility Multi-Wheeled Vehicle; more commonly known as a Humm-Vee
HVI .... High value individual
HVT .... High value target
HQ .... Headquarters
IA .... Iraqi Army
ICDC .... Iraqi Civil Defense Corps
IFV .... Infantry fighting vehicle; see M2 and M113
IED .... Improvised explosive device
IP .... Iraqi police
IR .... Infra-red
ISF .... Iraqi security forces
KIA .... Killed in action
LSA .... Logistics support area
MbiTR .... Small squad radio; literally a Mobile Broadband Individual Tactical Radio
MRE .... meal ready to eat
MNC-I .... Multi National Corps Iraq

MNF-I .... Multi National Forces Iraq
MRE.......................... Meal Ready to Eat; U.S. combat ration
MSR .... Main Supply Route
M88 .... Armored recovery vehicle
M1 .... Abrams Tank
M113 .... Infantry fighting vehicle without a turret, more lightly armored than a M2
M1025 .... Scout HMMWV; hard topped with a gun turret
M2 .... Infantry Fighting Vehicle-holds up to nine soldiers; could also refer to a .50 caliber machine gun
M4/M16.................... Rifle used by most U.S. soldiers in Iraq
NCO .... Non-commissioned officer; the backbone of the Army
OP .... observation post
ODA .... Operational detachment alpha; small special forces element
OH58/64................... Observation helicopter
OIF .... Operation Iraqi Freedom
Overwatch .... Maintaining observation of an area, normally in support of a maneuver element
PB............................. Patrol base; normally occupied by a company or smaller element, less amenities than a FOB
PKC.......................... Soviet era light machine gun
QRF.......................... Quick reaction force
RCT.......................... Route clearance team
REDCON .... Ready condition; REDCON 1 means an element is ready to move immediately

ROE .... Rules of engagement; the rules that delineate when a soldier can use lethal force
ROGER..................... Understand all; normally a radio transmission
RP .... Release point
RPG .... Rocket propelled grenade
SITREP..................... Situation Report
SP .... Start point
SOP........................... Standard operating procedures
TF or Task Force....... A battalion headquarters that has different types of units attached to it with the intent of forming an organization with a specific set of capabilities to perform a specific mission; for example, infantry and tank battalions were normally cross leveled into Task Forces so they each had some of the others capabilities- with one or more infantry companies being attached to an armor battalion task force and vice versa. In the book TF/Task Force and Battalion are used interchangeably and all refer to the same headquarters.
Terp .... Short for interpreter
Three Letter Agency.. One or a combination of several of the U.S. government's many three lettered agencies
TTP........................... Tactics, techniques and procedures
TOC .... Tactical Operations Center; where command and control of a unit takes place
UAV .... Unmanned aerial vehicle
VBIED...................... Vehicle borne IED
WIA.......................... Wounded in action

WILCO...................... Will comply; normally a radio transmission

LaVergne, TN USA
21 January 2011
213347LV00004B/19/P